Kowloon x. 81.

SOUVENIRS OF AUGUSTE BORGET

By the same author
CHINNERY: The Man and the Legend

SOUVENIRS OF

AUGUSTE BORGET

ROBIN HUTCHEON

A SCMP PUBLICATION

To Bea

Contents

FOREWORD

On connaît mieux Auguste Borget à Hongkong qu'en France. S'il n'a pas sombré dans l'oubli c'est plus en raison de son amitié avec Honoré de Balzac que d'un talent qui n'avait pourtant pas échappé au roi Louis-Philippe. Comment ce jeune homme que sa famille destinait à la banque a-t-il été tenté par les Amériques et l'Extrême-Orient? Comment n'a-t-il pas cédé à l'exotisme grandiloquent ou facile alors que le romantisme avait conquis l'Europe?

Chacune de ses oeuvres est un récit, rigoureux et fidèle.

A Canton, à Macao, à Hongkong, en pleine guerre de l'opium, Borget composait ses lithographies avec une sérieuse tranquillité. Comme s'il eut planté son chevalet dans sa campagne d'Issoudun. Témoin fidèle d'un temps qui n'était pas le sien.

Ses oeuvres reproduites sont répandues partout à Hongkong. Elles font partie de son patrimoine culturel sans que l'on sache assez qui est l'auteur.

Monsieur R.G. Hutcheon comble cette lacune. Son livre est le fruit d'une fervente recherche. Et surtout la rencontre de deux sensibilités : celle de Borget et celle d'un écrivain et journaliste, qui a vécu longtemps à Hongkong et compte parmi ceux qui peuvent ressusciter un esprit au détour de ses rues, les paysages d'hier.

Dès mon arrivée à Hongkong, M. R.G. Hutcheon m'avait fait partager son enthousiasme pour ce peintre français. Qu'il soit remercié et félicité d'offrir cette découverte aux lecteurs de cet ouvrage.

Et à ceux qui auront la nostalgie de ces harmonies anciennes, disons qu'elles survivent à quelques kilomètres de la ville. Dans ces villages des Nouveaux Territoires où s'offrent encore le reflet des tuiles vernissées, la racine tourmentée des banians, les grands éboulis de granits roses, et l'azur des baies piqué de voiles mandarines.

Yves Rodrigues
Consul General de France
Hongkong

SOTHEBY PARKE BERNET COLLECTION

Sold at auction, Hongkong,
December 4, 1978

Beaching a sampan in Mirs Bay

A street scene

Interior of a barber's shop

Fisherman and a junk near Hongkong

A street restaurant in Canton

Sampans on the shore, Macau

A beachcomber at Macau

A junk off the coast of China

Chinese girl from Su-Tien

A fruit seller in Macau

A barber in Macau

A scene in Macau

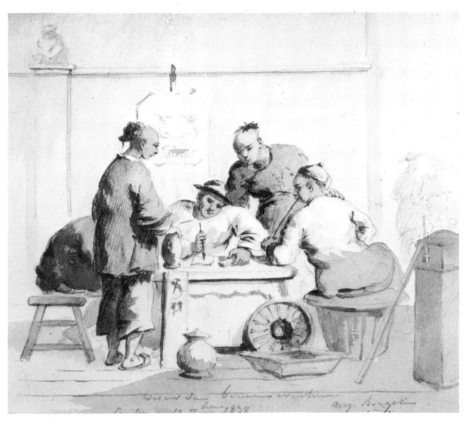

Letter writer in a Canton Street

Sampans on the shore

INTRODUCTION

ISSOUDUN, 130 miles south of Paris, has acquired over the centuries those qualities that its solid, worthy citizens value—dignity, respectability, stability, even a quiet and unostentatious charm. It lays no claim to fame (or infamy) and extremes and superlatives of any kind are conspicuous by their absence. The Romans settled and civilised it. Richard Coeur de Lion, interminably at odds with the French barony, built an observation tower on a small hill overlooking the town square which survives to this day. It once possessed a hospital, renowned centuries ago as a centre of care and healing, and today it is the town's museum straddling a sluggish, weed-choked stream. Within its walls are the scrappy chronicles of its dull and unremarkable past. There is also a collection of six drawings by an artist called Auguste Borget who dignified the town by being born there in 1808. But shaking off parental bonds, he left it as soon as he decently could to seek fame as an artist in Paris.

In an age when Delacroix and Ingres were at their height and romantic art the fashion, Borget's paintings and drawings were never likely to compete with the great masters for wall space in national museums— though they were good enough to win a gold medal at a provincial salon and catch the eye and open the purse of Louis-Philippe, King of the French.

Today, Borget is collected by smaller provincial museums, though in most cases to be stored away for a posterity that may never hear of him. A few experts remember him as a subtle and sensitive artist, better (and certainly more prolific) with the pencil and pastels than a paintbrush—though his few surviving paintings show that at his best he handled small canvases with great competence and a pleasing eye for design and colour.

He also achieved the distinction of being one of the most widely travelled artists of his time and his sketches gained him wider recognition among the French public than if he had confined his work to Europe. Others, however, might remember him less as the artist who brought back a fascinating collection of pictures of South America, the Sandwich Islands, China, the Philippines and India, than because of his relationship with one of the country's greatest 19th century novelists, Honoré de Balzac.

The interplay between his creative spirit, his vagabond nature, his compassionate outlook on life and his personal involvement with two close friends, forms the subject of this book.

We know him best as the artist who has left a series of attractive lithographs of Hongkong, Macau and Canton which became part of the Chater collection now residing in the Hongkong Museum of Art. These cover his stay during the years 1838–1839 and have been published as a series of 12 prints. In addition, he completed hundreds of drawings of various aspects of Chinese life and those that have been published show a skill of draughtsmanship, an eye for detail and a sense of liveliness that entitle him to be introduced to a wider public. Hence this book.

Because of the variety of pictures available, the emphasis is more on illustrations than text and selections of Borget's work done in various parts of the world have been included. Scenes of China, however, predominate.

The absence of notes to the text has meant that where necessary sources have been included in the narrative. Occasionally, in the course of his letters home, Borget uses the word *fanqui*—a term familiar to most foreigners who have lived in Hongkong and China, for it is one of the common epithets which the Chinese use to describe non-Chinese and particularly Westerners.

One meaning of the words (Borget joined the two together) is "foreign evil spirit" and this summed up pretty accurately in Chinese eyes the aggressive, rapacious Westerner when he first visited the country. Today, he is better known as a *kwai lo* (or "devil person"), suggesting that there has not been very much improvement in manners or behaviour in the last 500 years.

The title "Souvenirs" is taken from a criticism by the well-known French art critic Beaudelaire who said of his work in 1845: "No doubt they are very well done but they are regrettably too precisely souvenirs of a journey or accounts of customs." A trifle caustic, perhaps, but if we cannot place Borget in the highest ranks his pictures survive today as charming postcards and pleasing reproductions in many offices and homes. In that role he deserves to be remembered as a fine craftsman of great talent—and we are indebted to him for a variety of views that have not been bettered by any Western artist before, during or after his time.

In the chapters on Borget's visit to China, I have included extensive excerpts from his letters to France, as translated in the English edition of *Sketches of China and the Chinese*, and in some cases have taken small liberties with the punctuation and wording for the sake of fluency, but without changing the sense. Other excerpts have been taken from *Fragments d'un voyage autour du monde* and I have had to lean on French and Canadian friends to help polish my far from perfect translations. I can only conclude that Borget sounds very much better in his native language and I beg his forgiveness for any mistranslations which may have unwittingly crept in.

It was exciting that shortly before this book was published a number of interesting and hiterto unknown drawings and two oils by Borget came up in the December, 1978, sale of paintings by Sotheby's in Hongkong. I am indebted to Mr Julian Thompson and Mr Patrick Bowring for providing me with black and white photographs and coloured slides which appeared in the catalogue of Sotheby Parke Bernet (Hongkong) Ltd for the sale of their fine Chinese school and European pictures.

The emergence of Borget's paintings and drawings from private collections raises hope that these and perhaps others will throw more light on his life and particularly his voyage around the world. Regrettably, it has not been possible to do more than to include the photographs in this book.

I am indebted to many who have assisted me. These include Mr Geoffrey Bonsall, Director of the Hongkong University Press who read, amplified and corrected the manuscripts of a series of five articles which I wrote for the South China Morning Post in 1977; he also provided material and lent me his copy of *La Chine Ouverte*; Mr Francis Lothrop, Hon. Trustee, the Peabody Museum, Salem, Massachusetts, who drew my attention to Borget's pictures in the Peabody collection and assisted me in other ways; Mr H.A. Rydings, the Librarian, University of Hongkong, who allowed me to photograph pages of Borget's book *Sketches of China and the Chinese*; the British Council in Hongkong and Paris which helped me to obtain photocopies of Borget's second book *Fragments d'un voyage autour du monde* from the Bibliotheque Nationale in Paris; M. Yves Rodrigues, French Consul-General In Hongkong, who was a constant source of encouragement and was instrumental in bringing an exhibition of a number of Borget's works to Hongkong; Mr David Davies, Manager, Agence France Presse, Hongkong, who helped me track down a number of museums containing Borget's works, M. Pierre Furic of Paris who assisted me greatly with research; Mrs Michele Kay of Hongkong and Paris and Mr Patrick Jacquelin of London who helped with translations and investigations, and many others, not forgetting my constant source of inspiration and help, my wife, Bea.—RH

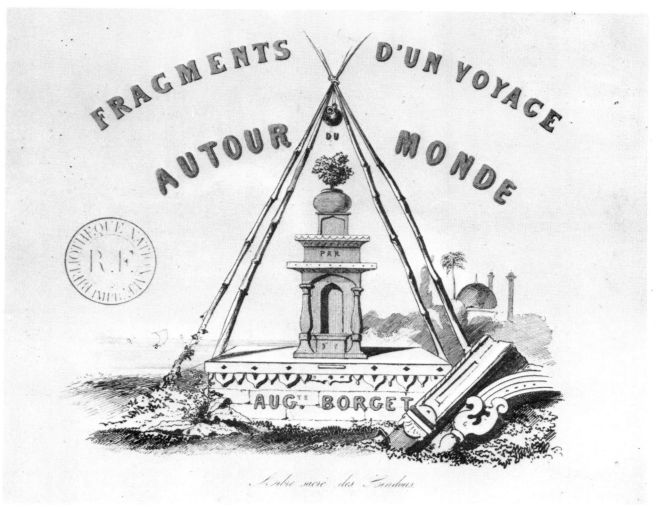

Frontispiece of Borget's book *Fragments d'un Voyage autour du Monde* entitled Sacred tree of the Hindus.

Windmills on the banks of the Hudson River, opposite New York.

The Cathedral of Notre Dame at Rio de Janeiro

Street scene in Buenos Aires

Street scene in Lima

Horses drinking at a fountain in Peru

Chilean horseman on the Santiago Plain

The bridge and town of Pasig in the Philippines

Calcutta street scene

Street and market at Canton

FRANCE

WELL-TO-DO parents generally have definite ideas about the careers which their sons should follow. Daughters are allowed more latitude. But not sons. Not in this century. Or in the last century. Or in the one before that. And when in 1826 in the French town of Issoudun, an 18-year-old schoolboy announced to his family, with long and honourable links with commerce, that he preferred sketching and painting to wholesaling and retailing, the inevitable conflict ensued.

Auguste Borget was one of four children of Jean-Baptiste Borget and Adelaide Sourisseau. He had become interested in art while studying at the high school in the nearby town of Bourges where his talents had been encouraged by a teacher named Boichard the elder. But people like the Borgets who lived among "the massive and richly furnished houses of merchants and bankers at Issoudun", drew a careful distinction between a mere pastime to while away the hours, and a solid dependable career.

Not only did they refuse his wish, but at the age of 18 he was sent to work at a bank and remained there until he came of age. That he persisted for three years was a credit to his determination to salvage something from the experience, as well as a laudable example of filial respect. And in retrospect, he would have acknowledged that the training gave him a sense of respect for the value of money, care in managing it and prudence in spending it which was to remain with him all his life.

At 21, in 1829, Auguste announced his retirement from the world of banking and shook off the stifling atmosphere of his home town—guaranteed, as his friend Balzac would later say, to have put Napoleon to sleep. There was probably agreement between the Borgets—father and son—that there were other and more acceptable ways of pursuing his new career than by starving in some wretched garret in the artists' quarter of Paris. The family therefore arranged for him to stay with old friends from Issoudun, Major Carraud and his wife, Zulma, whose father had signed Auguste's baptismal certificate.

This link was to propel the young and impressionable Auguste into a heady new existence which would bring him into contact with some of the city's most talked about people. This is how it happened. Major Carraud was an instructor at the St Cyr military academy and among his friends was an old school mate named Surville who had married a girl called Laure Balzac. Her brother, Honoré, was a rising young writer who used to visit the household where he met Madame Carraud and Auguste. They struck up a friendship —essentially a union of three like-minded and gifted people. Though Balzac was some nine years older than Borget, and three years younger than Zulma Carraud, they were bound by "a spirit of harmony, a love of beauty and a zest for life."

Zulma Carraud emerges as the most stable of the three. Borget was somewhat overwhelmed by his new environment but was delighted to have found like-minded friends in this exciting city. Balzac was the literary butterfly fluttering about in bursts of creative energy which established his reputation as a writer; he was at the same time an incurable spendthrift for ever trying to escape the cocoon of bankruptcy which sought to envelope him.

Like Borget, Balzac had suffered from a domineering family who saw a career in law as a more respectable way of making a living. He lasted three years at university, working as a clerk in a lawyer's office in his spare time. Balzac's family later relented, though not before his first literary efforts had earned a rebuke from a critic that he was wasting his time. Some of his early works, including novels written under a pseudonym, met with little success.

However, he was determined to persevere for he saw in himself the same spark of genius that he thought he detected in the young artist from Issoudun.

In 1829 he launched into a series of novels, *La Comédie Humaine*, which at one time was planned to number 143 works covering all aspects of 19th century French life. About 91 were completed before his death at the age of 51.

His writing eventually brought him fame but his love of luxury and his unbridled passions drove him deeper and deeper into debt. He set himself up as a publisher and bought a type foundry in 1827 but it sank like lead.

20

He was supported financially by his mother and a Madame de Berny, a god-daughter of Louis XVI and Marie Antoinette, and though 22 years his senior she was to give Balzac much of the affection and love he had missed as a child when he spent six years at school without seeing his family. Her death in 1836 was a time of profound grief for Balzac.

Balzac also saw in Borget a kindred spirit and in 1832, when he was writing *Louis Lambert*, their friendship matured and ripened to the point where Auguste moved into his apartment at I Rue Cassini, in Paris.

He wrote to Zulma Carraud: "I thank you for having given me such a good friend. His is a completely fraternal soul for me, full of attention that I love and I hope that I am for him everything that he is for me." Zulma Carraud replied: "I am happy about the tenderness of your relations with Auguste; his is indeed an exceptional soul."

In this new relationship, Borget shared in the triumphs of his friend's literary achievements but also experienced the remorse and sorrow into which Balzac was plunged by his torrid love life.

One letter from Balzac told Borget of his love for the dying Madame de Berny: "Oh my dear Auguste, I am writing to you with tears in my eyes. It was for her sake that I was in love with glory, fame . . ."

But this attachment did not prevent Balzac from having associations with the Duchesse d'Abrantes, the widow of one of Napoleon's marshals, and there were affairs, such as with the Marquise de Castries who had written him an admiring letter following publication of one of his works, and later with a Polish countess, Eveline Hanska.

It was upon the latter Balzac poured his unrestrained love until he married her six months before his death. Nor was this all; in 1834 there was an English woman, Sarah Lowell, and through her he bought a property at Villa d'Avray.

It is a mark of Borget's great understanding of and devotion to Balzac that he kept himself firmly in the background both developing his own style as an artist and perfecting his technique.

He became a pupil of Baron Jean-Antoine Gudin who excelled as a painter of seascapes and it was through him that he developed his talent for capturing the various moods of lakes, rivers and seas in many parts of the world.

He also felt the urge to travel. The Bay of Naples and the canals of Venice were favourite themes of Borget, still in his mid-20s, and he also made many chaik drawings of the Swiss lakes and the Dutch countryside.

A critic wrote: "In them he found the marriage of water and town and which he was destined to cherish later on, to the extent of not being able to tear himself away from the bays of Canton and Macau or the shores of the Ganges in India."

There were, however, doubts at this time whether Borget was as devoted to his art as a serious student should have been. Though he always went on his visits well equipped and came back with many drawings "he lived according to his whims, staying with friends in the country or undertaking in France and elsewhere so-called study trips".

It was in Switzerland that Borget was introduced by Balzac to the family of Madame Hanska. And it was Balzac who ordered his friend to burn their correspondence should he die.

"He has the blind fidelity of a dog," wrote Balzac of Borget. The Hanskas "liked him tremendously."

When Balzac died, all but two of Madame Hanska's letters were burnt as requested, though Balzac's correspondence was published years after his death in two volumes under the title of *Lettres a l'Etrangere*.

Balzac, now at the height of his creative power, was to publish some of his best works in the next few years. Ever impecunious and spendthrift, he borrowed heavily from friends including Borget, and when he failed to repay the loan but bought himself a gold penknife instead, he received a gentle rebuke from his young friend.

"I am not worth very much," wrote Borget, "but really, tell me why all this brilliant luxury of which you speak. Wasn't the situation I left you in enough?"

Later he delivered some "words of harsh truth" and accused Balzac of egoism and frivolously spending his advance payment of rights amounting to 10,000 francs.

It was less a symptom of a cooling friendship, however, than a measure of Borget's frankness. Balzac was at this time leading a hectic social life which kept the friends apart often, and Borget found his consolation increasingly in travel.

About the middle of 1836, he decided to leave France for a visit to the United States, South America and the Orient despite fervent appeals from his family in Issoudun, Zulma Carraud and Balzac.

In a letter to Balzac. Madame Carraud wrote: "I told Auguste not to undertake the voyage in question. He is losing his time. He refuses to see that there is a technique to be mastered in the arts. In literature, in painting, in music, in sculpture, 10 years of work are required before one understands the synthesis of the art-medium at the same time as the analysis of the art-matter.

"One is not a great painter because one has seen many countries, strange people, etc; one can copy a tree and create a tremendous masterpiece. It would have been better for him to struggle for two years with light and colour, sitting at home like Rembrandt who never left his house, than to go off to America in order to bring back the cruel disillusionment about political matters which he is certain to bring back."

Zulma Carraud was a shrewd and perceptive observer and her insight proved right.

Borget was, however, less the committed artist at this stage of his life than a dedicated traveller and a student of human existence, having broken away from a career in banking to see the world. He must have been acutely aware of his own limitations as an artist, his want of technique and experience, his restless, inquiring spirit. He could not be tied to his easel and his studio. Moreover, though his friendship with and devotion for Balzac had brought a new excitement to his previously sheltered existence, Borget felt his destiny demanded something more than Paris and even Europe could offer..

He began preparations for a trip that was to last almost four years and was to result in an outpouring of his sensitive and artistic talent in copious letters, drawings and paintings.

22

PEABODY MUSEUM
SALEM, MASSACHUSETTS

A selection of Borget's sketches

A river scene near Honolulu

Houses and palms, Honolulu

A beach hut near Honolulu

Outrigger canoes near Honolulu

Ruins in Manila

Interior of a house in Honolulu

THE AMERICAS

WHEN AUGUSTE BORGET announced his intention to travel around the world, his friends told him the enterprise was risky, unwise and inimical to his future as an artist. Their pleas, however, failed to deter him. His passion for travel had already been stirred by his tours of Europe and, seven years after beginning his new career, Borget must have taken stock of his prospects and concluded a change of scenery might do more for his reputation than languishing in Paris as the lapdog of an increasingly famous novelist.

Like many young artists, Borget believed he might gain fresh inspiration by travelling abroad. Possibly he had noticed the change in the work of Eugène Delacroix after he visited Morocco and Spain in 1832, and believed that he too might acquire an exotic influence from an overseas visit. Determination, self-assertion, but above all, a keen desire to make his own way in life, motivated the young artist.

And while it is apparent that he enjoyed some independent means, possibly from his family, to undertake the world tour required more than his present income.

There are hints in correspondence that he made the trip to New York at no great expense but his brief banking career had given him a good understanding of business methods and Borget was in no doubt that he could cover his costs at each stage.

He joined up with a young companion named Guillon whose father was an exporter in Le Havre. Their ship sailed on October 25, 1836, and Borget wrote that his "heart was dilated by joy and his head was aflame." After a crossing lasting more than a month they arrived in New York early in December. Almost immediately Borget, an indefatigable correspondent, was describing the excitement of his arrival in a letter to his widowed mother in Issoudun.

He lodged in "an immense hotel where three or four hundred people eat and sleep every day. The hotel is a vast place. The dining room holds 800 people."

He apologised for not writing earlier. "In the bedrooms, there is nothing but a bed, a table and a chair, no inkstand, no pen, nothing. The Americans leave fully dressed in the morning and return home in the evening at bedtime, and as they need no such things, there are none . . .

"We are learning English as fast as we can in order to head for the backlands where we will find very few people able to understand us.

"I shall not speak about the crossing, dear Mother, I was sick but not as much as I thought I would be; we had a storm or a strong wind at least once a week. We withstood some very violent ones . . . The American ships are so well built that there is nothing to fear except along the coasts; on the high seas during a frightful storm, when the waves were dashing over the deck, the captain told me—and it's the truth—that we were in less danger than we would be on the road from Paris to Rouen.

"So here I am, safe and sound. But it is nine o'clock: I am going to an American ball tonight and my friends are waiting for me ... we have found other compatriots here who have been extremely kind. Farewell, Mother, I kiss you all and love you with all my heart."

Another letter was sent to Zulma Carraud, who then wrote to his friend the novelist Honoré de Balzac, to say: "I am afraid, just as you are, that he will bring back a number of disappointments from this New World; everything he sees surprises him; the manners which are so different, so positive, so free, hurt him beyond reason. He has already made many acquaintances because of his talent as an artist. It is very possible that this trip may not bear all the fruit that he expects from it; but one can easily understand the attraction which such an excursion had for him and, especially at so little expense. It was an opportunity which does not occur twice in a lifetime, and although I am sorry to see him so far away from us, I cannot disapprove of his action."

It seems from letters that in New York Borget was employed in some way for he refers occasionally to his "boss" but while his work took up most of his time during the week, Sundays would often find him on the banks of the Hudson River sketching.

A drawing made shortly after his arrival shows a windmill on the river bank with a number of sailing ships nearby. The picture would later find its way into a book of lithographs entitled *Fragments d'un voyage autour du monde* which Borget published nine years later.

In the accompanying text he conveyed his excitement at living in New York. He wrote: "Located at the lower end of the little island of Manhattan, between the East River—full of ships from all corners of the universe—and the Hudson—that magnificent river without rival in Europe—New York is assuredly one of the most beautiful, one of the most finely built, one of the richest and most industrious cities in the world. Its almost fabulous growth, its constantly mounting wealth, make it one of the most interesting spots on the globe to study ...

"On Sundays, the newcomer finds it difficult to get used to the complete silence which follows the extraordinary bustle of the other days of the week. One would think that the plague had invaded the city and that all of its inhabitants had deserted it on the same day and the very same hour; not an omnibus, not a carriage.

"The wharves which were swarming with life are deserted, and if some passerby ventures forth on Broadway, he hides as best he can, slipping along past the walls as though he were afraid of being seen, identified and ostracised.

"I made use of this inhospitable day to cross over to the right bank of the Hudson, to the New Jersey fields, in search of a less disheartening sight than that of a city without its inhabitants. It was only upon returning from a delightful walk that I stopped, in Hoboken, before getting back on the boat, to sketch a windmill which stands on the river bank between this town of summer residences belonging to fortunate New Yorkers, and the little city of Jersey."

But his stay in New York was shortlived—possibly due to a cold winter which he was not prepared for. One biographer estimates the date of his departure as January 1837, which would have meant a stay of about six weeks.

For the next two months Borget and his companion, Guillon, were at sea, each day getting warmer and longer as winter gave way to summer in the southern hemisphere. Their first stop was Brazil and the ship dropped anchor in the bay of Rio de Janeiro. The change, offering as it did a blazing sun, exotic birds, colourful flowers and an abundance of lush trees and vegetation, fascinated him.

The one blight which he was quick to condemn was the ill-treatment of slaves. "Why, beneath such a beautiful sky, must there be so many unfortunate blacks who are suffering? Everywhere in the streets, on the public squares, on the shore, I see poor negroes staggering under crushing loads, while their backs, furrowed by the whip, are evidence of the unmitigated harshness of their masters."

He has left us pictures of the lively spirited people who filled the streets of Rio, in contrast to the gangs of slaves chained by the neck being marched to work.

No less revolting than the treatment of the slaves was the cruelty by the Creoles to the Indians of the Pampas. The two travellers moved on quickly to Montevideo, taking the British mail steamer, *Spider*, and then trans-shipping to the Argentinian schooner, *Rosa*, to sail to Buenos Aires.

There Borget was impressed by the opulence of the beautiful shops, the richly ornamented horses of the gauchos and the fine garments of the womenfolk returning from church, "followed at a distance by a small negro slave who carries the carpet on which you kneel down to pray."

But while struck by the wealth of the city, the sad state of the countryside depressed the French travellers and Borget gave vent to a bitter tirade against the way the country was run.

Argentina was then under a reign of terror by the xenophobic tyrant Juan Manuel de Rosas; less than five years earlier Charles Darwin on his round-the-world voyage of exploration on HMS Beagle had met Rosas and his hard-living, hard-drinking, rough and ready gaucho cavalrymen. Rosas then greeted Darwin with courtesy and charm, though the proceedings were grave and formal throughout—just as well, since Rosas was said to be most dangerous when he laughed.

He had little hesitation in having his own men shot or tortured. He demanded standards of ruthlessness, fitness and courage that could only be found among the gauchos. Rosas could ride a wild horse bareback to a stand-still and demanded the same test of horsemanship of his men.

The terrible massacres inflicted on the Indians shocked Darwin. He wrote in his diary that the Christian soldiers under Rosas' command were far more savage than the helpless pagans they were destroying.

Yet Rosas' men were convinced this was the only solution if Argentina was to be made safe for the cattle and sheep ranchers who were settling the country. They therefore treated them all—men, women and children—as criminals. Darwin tried remonstrating to save the women but Rosas' henchmen considered them worse than vermin—"they breed so fast".

When Borget rode through the countryside conditions had undoubtedly worsened and even European settlers and merchants had complained about the wild and desperate men serving under Rosas' command. But the white man's afflictions were nothing compared with the misery imposed on the Indians.

Borget wrote: "Do people believe that news of the massacre of the Aztecs and of the sons of the Incas has not reached them? No matter how intense their isolation may be, it is not of such a nature as to have prevented them from learning of the fate of the 60 Indians from the banks of the Uruguay who were sent, not more than a month ago, from Santa Fe to Buenos Aires, and who were shot on the very day of their arrival, near a broad ditch which had been dug in advance to receive their corpses.

"What would they say if they knew that one of these wretches, while feeling the first spadeful of dirt fall on him, rose up all of a sudden like a ghost from the midst of this heap of dead bodies, all gory with his own blood and that of his brothers, and shouted: 'I am a Christian!'

"By what name would they call us if they knew that the person who was supervising this butchery climbed down into the ditch, walked over the bodies, and as his only answer ripped open the belly of the poor resurrected Indian?

"Upon recalling this infamous slaughter, the more curses I heard against our assailants, the more just their cause appeared to me."

The bitterness of his words was fully matched by the despondency of the people depicted in his drawings, yet the image presented by one writer of Borget as a delicate, mild-mannered, easily shocked traveller does him no credit.

To have attempted this journey, fraught as it was with a large number of uncertainties not the least of which were hostile Indians, suggests a man of great courage. He was to record his experiences and emotions in a long article on his return to France entitled *Dans Les Pampas* which he wrote in Cordoba in May of 1837 after a 400-mile crossing of the plain.

Borget and his companion Guillon then continued their trek through the rugged "lost provinces" southwest of Cordoba to Mendoza. He described in one of his books the ordeal: "eight days after leaving Cordoba and saying goodbye to our friends and compatriots, our caravan advanced slowly into an unknown region through which our guides gropingly led us. We reached the summit of an immense plateau, sad and mournful, where the tall marsh grass into which we disappeared cut out the sunshine. . . .

". . . We found ourselves all of a sudden in front of a perpendicular precipice which extended in a straight line as far as we could see. It was only after a long search by our guides that we were able to discover not so much a path as a passage by which, thanks to several rocky outcrops, our mules, relieved of their loads and their riders no less burdened than they, could descend.

"But at the foot of the precipice, more than 80 feet below, the going was far worse. The undergrowth was so impenetrable, so compacted by creepers which entwined themselves around trees that to clear a path we had to use hatchets and knives, until at last we reached a spot where the trees thinned out. This allowed us a complete view of the rocks we had to cross to leave this endless cliff, the serenity of which I am sure could only rarely have been disturbed by the voice of man."

This exhausting journey compelled them to break for almost three weeks in Mendoza to recover their strength. But winter was now fast approaching and this meant either a prolonged stay in this hospitable far western outpost of Argentina or a crossing of the Andes in icy conditions. Borget chose to move on and for a week they experienced bitter cold, passing through mountainous country of up to 11,000 feet.

Two years earlier, Charles Darwin, making this same trek, wrote about riding for hour after hour through the icy wind, fighting for breath at high altitudes and at certain points on the ridges, having to stop every 50 yards because of the rarefied air.

Darwin made his passage in March, as autumn was beginning. Borget made his crossing in July, in midwinter, and although shelters were available part of the way, on one night they had to sleep under a large rock shelf. A week later they emerged unscathed through the Uspallata pass, with its magnificent view of the valley of Santa Rosa de Los Andes below, and entered Chile.

The terrors of Argentina behind him, Borget, succumbed to the pleasures of Chile. "If a place on earth exists, a world where my journey might have ended," he wrote, "that place is Chile; and if having left France once again, I were destined to go to South America to live, it is toward Chile that I would instinctively set my course.

"My preference for the country, the republic which certainly has before it the greatest future among all the nations of the New World, is perhaps due solely to the misery and suffering which I went through while crossing the immense chain of the Andes in the midst of winter, to the discomforts which did not end until we entered the beautiful valley of Santa Rosa de Los Andes.

"But for life to move pleasantly along and pass away gently, is it not sufficient that one has a beautiful sky, healthy air, happy valleys and kindly welcoming people?"

The two travellers spent six and a half months in the region of Santiago and Valparaiso. It was in Chile, moreover, that Borget apparently gave up whatever business commitments he had and took a new and more serious interest in his art, in the company of another young and prominent Bavarian artist, Johann Moritz Rugendas.

Like Borget, Rugendas had left his native country to travel through South America and it is said that he exerted a strong influence on the development of the Frenchman's technique as a draughtsman.

If his artistic output in Santiago was slight, the Valparaiso era is one of the most flourishing and productive in Borget's long voyage. It was in that city that Rugendas had his studio, and it led to a close friendship between the two men.

Found in Borget's protfolios years later were four original drawings by Rugendas dated 1837, one of which was a pencil portrait of Borget. In addition, there was a large number of tracings on yellow paper by Borget based on drawings by Rugendas.

Why did he make these tracings? Borget has left us no explanation, but a lifelong weakness was his difficulty in drawing people and animals. As his biographer. David James, has said: "The lack of human forms in his Brazilian and Argentine drawings or the insufficient knowledge of human anatomy which they reveal, represent an inferiority which must have cut into Borget's artistic sensitivity sharply."

Rugendas' skill as an artist has been likened to that of Ingres, one of France's greatest painters of the last century, and Borget could have found no more inspiring example in this part of the world to help him remedy this serious flaw in his technique.

It was Rugendas who provided the stimulus to work on this weakness and helped him to achieve form and movement in his work, even if the detail still betrayed an uncertainty and lack of confidence.

Rugendas left Chile in December of 1837 on an expedition to Argentina where he stayed for several months. It was time, too, for Borget to move on and, after continuing drawing in the area of Valparaiso for another two months, he finally boarded the *Henry Clay*, a Yankee packet boat bound via ports for China.

It was a journey that would take him to northern Chile, Bolivia and Peru before crossing the Pacific to the Sandwich Islands, the Moluccas, the Philippines and then Macau.

Before leaving South America he visited several small ports where he recorded his impressions in word and picture.

He tells us: "I visited Tacna, watered three times a week by a torrent which pours into another valley on the other days. I was present at the noisy carnival festivities and saw the dishevelled and indescribable dances that accompany them. I crossed the threshold of more than one Indian dwelling in which the inhabitants still wear mourning for their last Inca."

At Islay he was so fascinated by all he saw that "during all the time my hand did not remain idle and my pencil did not rest for a single instant. Flocks of llamas either pack-laden or sleeping in the shade; Indians with their little striped ponchos, their strange head-dress, their long straight hair, and their yellow faces, indolent and resigned; rich facades of churches, interiors of houses, humble dwellings of cotton-spinners with their wheel turned by a little trickle of water—I sketched everything not forgetting the volcano which was often clouded with smoke."

The visit to Chile and Peru and his meeting with Rugendas had been one of the most inspiring, satisfying and prolific periods of his entire tour so far but his regret at tearing himself away from these surroundings was more than matched by a burning curiosity to discover what lay on the other side of the Pacific.

There are also indications that one of Borget's travelling companions died, though precisely where and when is not known. He alluded to the passing of his friend called Jacquemont in one of his China letters but in such a way as to suggest that this had occurred before reaching the Orient.

In a letter from the Bay of Hongkong on August 23, 1838, in which he describes a burial scene, he wrote that "it brought to my mind the sorrowful fate of poor Jacquemont, dying even at the port from which he was about to sail, to return to his country, his relations, and his family, who already spoke of his return, and perhaps even received a letter from him in the very moment when he expired. This indeed is the sting of absence. The letter which we read, after dilating our heart for a moment, leaves it full of doubts and inquietudes, for time in its course may bring many events; and frequent have been my struggles with such ideas I assure you . . ."

How much this event influenced his movements we do not know, but having reached the west coast of South America Borget's adventurous spirit and inquiring mind must have convinced him that there was only way to return to France.

LA CHINE OUVERTE

A selection of Borget's illustrations
for "La Chine Ouverte"
by old Nick

The Emperor

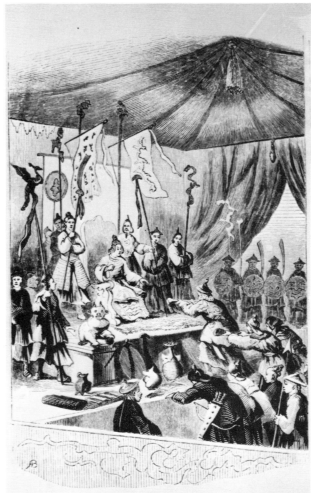

Presenting tribute to the Emperor

The Great Wall, Peking

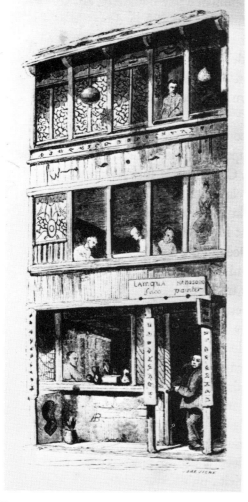

Lamqua's studio

Civil service examinations

Theatre scene

A scholar presents himself to his examiner

Captured pirates after a battle

Disgraced mandarin takes his leave

Prisoner in the stocks

Chinese soldiers in training

A mandarin's boat

The old curio shop

Old China street, Canton

Western merchants supervises unloading of merchandise

Market scene

Selling poultry in the market

Making lacquer

Tea picking

Chinese rural waterwheel

Cricket fighting

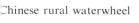

Drying tea leaves

A group of beggars

Ear cleaning

THE CHINA COAST

THE SEA JOURNEY from Peru to Canton, lasting almost four months, and taking in the Hawaiian islands, was a time of reflection and refreshment for Auguste Borget during his world tour.

Every day offered him a wealth of new scenes as the mood of the sea changed with the winds that carried the *Henry Clay* across the Pacific. Surviving pictures include pastels and a gouache of the moon rising in the mist on Sunday, May 18, 1838. A week later his vessel dropped anchor off Honolulu and Borget spent four days on the beaches of Oahu and in the town itself, determined to capture as much of the enchanting tropical scenery as time allowed.

But Borget was also a keen observer of the way of life of the Hawaiian people who were at that time coming under increasing attention from western, and particularly American, missionaries. He noted that while the Hawaiian King's palace was almost in ruins, the wretched huts of the natives were gradually giving way to comfortable white houses.

Where was it heading, he asked? "God grant that those who are charged with leading these childish people to the age of man, achieve their great mission. But alas, I hope that these simple and primitive beings who live on the shore by this beautiful sea in their modest dwellings at the foot of coconut groves, will not have to pay dearly for their too rapid initiation into the European way of life, and that our civilisation does not kill them off as it has killed the Indians of South America."

On July 14, 1838, the *Henry Clay* finally left the islands, at that time still known to mariners as the Sandwich Islands, so named by Captain James Cook 50 years earlier in honour of the then First Lord of the Admiralty, the Earl of Sandwich. It took a course for the Moluccas and the Philippines, and in August it ran into a typhoon. Borget had been nervous about the rough seas he encountered in the Atlantic but the China Sea proved to be a far more intimidating experience though he and his ship emerged unscathed.

Before visiting Canton and Macau, Borget trans-shipped to the French frigate *Psyche* for a voyage along the Kwangtung and Fukien coast, travelling up to Amoy. And in a letter written on board the *Psyche* on August 9, 1838, he said: "I am then at last in China. I have taken possession of the Celestial Empire! And fortunately without experiencing what generally accompanies long-expected pleasures—expectation has detracted nothing from the reality. I am as proud of it as if it were a conquest."

The rigours of ship life and the salt-water baths could be put aside. When they reached the island of Nam O (near Swatow) the captain invited him not only to the luxury of a walk ashore after four months at sea, but to bathe in fresh water.

Borget wrote: "We landed in a creek where a pretty rivulet descends from the neighbouring heights watering in its course hundreds of little patches of earth planted with rice and sweet potatoes . . . for there is not an inch of ground that is not turned to account."

He later described rowing ashore to visit a valley—"a delightful little oasis spreading forth its charms of colour and of vegetation in the midst of arid mountains.

"There is nothing, it is true, very remarkable in all this; but either from prejudice or because the country is really unlike every other, I found in the landscape an air of strangeness which charmed me"—though not all of it for he commented later: "although as an artist, I dislike their rice fields, I could not help admiring the skill with which they distribute over them the scanty supply of water, but for which any harvest would be impossible, and all their labour vain."

Borget met a villager standing at a cottage door who "advanced towards us and received us with the greatest hospitality." Seated under the bower which shaded the door of the cottage Borget sketched the scene, then climbed the hill opposite to inspect an old fort which he scathingly ridiculed for its wooden guns, its population of hens and profusion of kitchen instruments . . . "it is a place of no importance for the island has nothing to fear but it serves well to exemplify the genius of a people to whom the letter of the law is everything and who conform themselves to rules and not to ideas . . ."

He tells us that the "battlemented walls" were "about five feet in thickness" and "all round are little buildings, probably the barracks for soldiers. On the left, under the shade of an immense tree, sat several Chinese, some of whom wore a half-military dress.

"At one end stands the house of the commandant, beneath the gateway leading to which sat a venerable old man, engaged in mending nets; and to my great surprise, knowing as I did the repugnance of the Orientals to have their portraits taken, he allowed me to sketch him . . ."

Two weeks later, Borget was in the bay of Hongkong, and after a day of showers "the sky cleared up and everything betokened a fine eveing. Perceiving on a part of the island opposite the city of Cow-loon, some fine trees which had hitherto escaped our notice and above which rose columns of blue smoke, I intimated my desire to visit the spot, and all the remonstrances of the patron could not dissuade me.

"After crossing some rice fields, separated from each other by little ditches, which serve at once to collect and distribute the necessary moisture, I found myself approaching a herd of buffaloes, under the care of some children, and I was glad to escape from the fierce looks with which they regarded me as they rolled about in the dirty pool in which they were recreating themselves, and which warned me that I must not expect from them the same forbearance that I had received from their masters.

"It is by no means unusual for these animals, although quite inoffensive to the Chinese, to discover an European, even when dressed in the native costume, and to attack him fiercely.

42

"Proceeding along a pathway, shaded by beautiful trees and magnificent clumps of bamboo all covered with creeping plants, I at length reached the village. Three parallel streets, about six feet in width, lead to the place or principal part of the village, the other end of which opens into a wide and well-paved street, at the top of which stands a large and fine building, more ornamented than any of the neighbouring houses, and probably the residence of the Mandarin."

At this village—possibly Wong Nei Chong—he was followed by a large crowd "which increased every minute, and all the inhabitants came to their doors to see the *fanqui* pass."

There "every one invited me to come in, offering me tea or a pipe. I entered into one of the houses, and after drinking some tea without sugar, from very small cups, the owner, an old man, begged me with the greatest appearance of cordiality, to accept the pipe from which I had been smoking.

"Indeed if I am everywhere received so well in this new world, I certainly shall have no reason to join in chorus with those who proclaim it the most inhospitable country on earth."

On leaving this village, he climbed a little hill which overlooked it and which commanded a view of all other parts of the valley—possibly the area now known as Happy Valley. "The view was very fine," wrote Borget. "At my feet spread out fields of green rice. On my left, I could perceive many little hamlets embosomed amongst fine large trees. On my right were some steep rocks, while in the distance and, terminating the view, appeared the bay and the fine mountains of Cow-Loon."

He then went on to describe a primitive water supply system in a part of the valley "which has only a narrow opening to the sea-shore. In the middle of this little gorge stands a large mass of rock, of which the inhabitants, with their usual persevering industry, have most skilfully availed themselves. On the summit they have formed a little canal, and placing at each extremity a pipe formed of bamboo, have thus constructed an aqueduct to convey the water across the valley, and so fertilised places which, without such an expedient, had been condemned to eternal sterility."

The next day, still in Hongkong, he landed "on the north-east, close by a promontory where there are several houses, to which are attached wheels for the purpose of withdrawing the fishing nets, which gave to the place quite a peculiar character. When I reached the spot I found the inhabitants engaged in taking up the nets, which they do very slowly, in order not to frighten the fish. When the nets were out of the water, they went in boats to fetch the fish, which they probably wanted for breakfast, for no sooner did they reach the shore than they immediately began to fry them, and to cook the rice, which they use instead of bread.

"The Chinese indeed, display remarkable skill in the preparation of these two dishes—their only food.

"The rice was so fine, so white, so firm, and the fish so fresh that I felt a great desire to taste it." He was invited to join them and soon he was "seated on the grass, beside the family, with a supply of fish in one little saucer, rice in another, and in each hand a little stick, of which I found it impossible to make any use.

"My entertainers were much amused at my awkwardness, for they were ignorant of the use of the spoon and the fork, supplying their places with these little sticks which they not infrequently cut from the nearest tree, and handle with the greatest dexterity.

"My European breakfast, composed of cold fowl, bread and a few slices of ham, greatly delighted the children who speedily devoured it. After breakfast I began to sketch, and my new friends surrounded me, everybody offering me their long pipes.

"When I had finished I rose and continued my walk towards a little cottage near the water, which I had previously observed on my way to the island of Won-Chon-Chow. As I approached, the dogs barked, the children began to cry and one old woman fairly took to her heels. I was surprised at this reception, so different from what I had been accustomed to.

"At length, however, everything became quiet and I advanced to the widest part of the street, and stationing myself opposite the temple, under an immense tree, whose roots stretched out on every side, I commenced sketching, and was soon surrounded by gazers, all anxious to see what I was about.

"One women, shorter than the others, and not being able to see over their heads, adopted an ingenious device to gratify her curiosity. Bringing a chair for me to sit upon, she placed herself close beside me, and took care to keep the crowd at a distance. She afterwards took me affectionately by the arm to conduct me to her house, touching first my breast and then her own, to explain to me that she would feel greatly honoured by my visit.

"I went with her accordingly, accompanied by as many of the crowd as the house could contain. They seated me on a large old-fashioned chair, the picture of one of the middle ages. Every one seemed anxious to serve me; one brought me tea, another *sham-show*, a third a sugared liquor, made of I know not what, but very insipid, which they offered to me, pointing to the perspiration which stood on my forehead, to intimate that it would refresh me."

Borget went on to describe the room to which he was taken: "It was about ten or twelve feet square, and without a roof. On the left side of the door stood the chair on which I sat, and on each side were shelves, on which were ranged common earthen ware dishes and jars filled with water. At the end stood a bench crowded with visitors. In one part of the wall was an opening of about a foot in depth, in which was hung a wooden frame, slightly gilt, containing a religious subject, before which stood vases of artificial flowers, little wax lights, and joss-sticks; all round were slips of yellow and red coloured paper on which were inscriptions, probably charms...."

The next day, Borget said he "crossed the bay and landed in a little creek, where there is a village of boats drawn ashore, a kind of habitation of which we have no idea in Europe, even in the poorest countries. Some of these boat-houses are sheltered under large trees, others lean against the rocks, but the greater part rest on the ground, supported by stays.

"The richer sort are placed on pieces of wood driven into the earth, and are generally augmented by another apartment, if we may so style a little enclosure surrounded by planks, and covered with a straw or cane roof, supported by four bamboos, and so arranged as to leave sufficient space between it and the planks to afford free admittance to the air and the light. These *holes* serve to accommodate five or six inhabitants, who are crowded together in a space in which a couple of Europeans could not exist."

44

Further on he witnessed a funeral. He wrote: "I perceived some children engaged in burning little slips of paper, while a priest—such at least I took him to be—was muttering prayers over them. Close at hand stood a tall bamboo, from the top of which hung a long slip of red silk about six inches wide, and covered with gold letters—a sort of banner which probably did not at all times occupy that situation.

"One of the villagers had just died, and they were performing the last sad duties; at a little distance in a miserable boat, supported by pieces of rock, sat an old man gazing upon the ceremonies with the utmost impassibility, thinking perhaps that it would soon come to his turn, and that death would put an end to his misery. Nothing around him showed any signs of a family; he seemed to be alone in the world, no child to gladden his solitary habitation, or to receive his last sigh, and to close his eyes. . . .

"At a little distance from the spot which death had so recently visited, but where I saw no tears shed, were seated groups of people; some engaged in cooking, and others in gaming:—here pleasure, there death, if not mourning! Whence proceeds this callousness? Is it want of affectionate sympathy, or seems to them such a life more a burden than a blessing? And do they suppose that once delivered from it there is no more cause for sorrow? To see these poor people, it is indeed not difficult to understand why they shed no tears over him who exchanges the hard fate to which their birth and their civilisation condemn them, for the asylum which the earth offers with eternal repose!

"This death without tears grieved me."

Still in Hongkong, he wrote of a "a place which I daily visit, but of which I believe I have not yet spoken. It is a neck of land which separates the two bays. The captains of the ships go thither to take exercise, or to repose themselves after the labours of the day; and the Chinese have there established a little building-yard, where they repair their boats.

"I have even there seen some pretty little schooners building, and the captains who furnish the plans and look after the execution of the work are charmed with the skill of the Chinese carpenters.

"A floating village has stationed itself round the building-yard, and a numerous population lives in the incredible number of boats of which the village is composed. At first there were only gambling and other disreputable houses, and a theatre. By and by, other boats arrived and joined the congregation, till at length the village assumed its present formidable size.

"Licentiousness and immorality unfortunately prevail to a fearful extent . . . Sometimes a war-junk or a mandarin-boat comes to investigate the state of the population; but they content themselves with going through the formalities of inspection, and depart, leaving everything as bad as before."

These were the fragmentary impressions that Borget has left us of Hongkong in 1838, then a remote, sparsely populated island visited occasionally by foreign sailing ships to take on water and perhaps fresh vegetables and food, but also showing signs of how it might develop in future—as a ship-building centre and an area for rest, recreation and shelter for ships in times of stress and storm.

If the decaying Ching dynasty in faraway Peking, or even Canton, were aware of its potential, they showed no sign of it. It was just one more routine port of call for a visiting mandarin.

Bridge near Canton

Bamboo aqueduct, Hongkong

Old temple and Chinese fort, island of Nam O

Courtesy: Hongkong and Shanghai Bank

Triumphal arch on the river between Macau and Canton
Courtesy: Hongkong and Shanghai Bank

A general view of Macau

Courtesy: Hongkong and Shanghai Bank

Bay and island of Hongkong

Courtesy: Hongkong and Shanghai Bank

Dessiné d'après nature par Aug. BORGET, lith par Eug. CICERI.   Imp Lemercier, Benard et C.ᵉ   MAISON DE MANDARIN SUR LES CANAUX DE MACAO A CANTON

A mandarin's mansion on the river between Macau and Canton
Courtesy: Hongkong and Shanghai Bank

Burial scene, China

The Great Temple of Macao

Village scene, China

Families on the move
Courtesy: French Exhibition of Books and Art, Hongkong, 1978

Village square, Hongkong

Pagoda near Canton

CANTON

WITH THE ARRIVAL of autumn Borget applied to visit Canton when the city was opened to foreign merchants for the trading season, much as it is now for the twice yearly trade fairs.

His first letter was dated September 9, 1838, and he travelled up-river from Macau during the day, arriving just as dusk fell.

He wrote: "In entering the river of Hong-Shang, we had to use our oars, for there was not a breath of wind. Daylight began to fail, and the approach of night grieved me as much as if it had been an unlooked for or unusual event. I was chagrined at the idea of passing, without seeing it, a country where there was so much to excite my imagination; and whenever I perceived the tall dark outline of a tower or a pagoda standing out against the sky, I was vexed at not being able to sketch it, and almost cursed the slow progress of time. At last day broke as we cast anchor before the Custom House. I could scarcely see it, yet I had my album in my hand ready to sketch it as soon as it should become sufficiently visible."

He wrote of the thrill of seeing a new city. "My companions, wearied out or indifferent, were still asleep long after I had commenced operations. By degrees the noise of awakening multitudes became more distinct, and boats began to arrive in great numbers.

"By and by, many pushed off from the shore, and so great was the movement in the part of the river where we were stationed, that I took it for the market place of the city, which stretches itself on both sides of the river. The most important part, situated on the left bank, is built on a hill, crowned by a fine tall pagoda.

"The houses of the city in general have only one storey, the windows of which open sometimes on elegant balconies, and sometimes on terraces covered with flowers. The love of flowers gives me a high opinion of the manners and the domestic happiness of the inhabitants."

Everything Borget saw prompted him to jot down an impression or observation either in words or in a sketch. He comments on the language, customs, colours and architecture.

"Many of the little balconies have columns and trellises painted in different colours. We Europeans think that there is no architectural beauty where other colours than white are introduced, and I suspect that the custom of painting everything, even to the roof, would not please us much; nevertheless there results from this diversity of colours a certain gaiety which gives to the Chinese towns much more animation than ours."

As his ship proceeded up-river, Borget continued with the description. "Almost immediately I perceived, surrounded by fields of rice and a magnificent clump of trees, a strange-looking city quite different from any we had yet seen.

"The roofs of the houses were flat and the gables built in fantastic forms. We proceeded onwards and everywhere most charming landscapes met our view: green hills crowned by little pagodas which seemed placed there expressly to look down upon the infinite number of boats which pass before them, for the movement is incessant."

The scenes of canals and waterways that branch off from the main stream intrigued Borget and he produced a series of sketches of the graceful buildings in their setting of trees and bamboos as he travelled along to Canton.

Here there was a mandarin's house; there a bridge; a temple; over there, a triumphal arch; a pagoda; a fort—and he sketched this Oriental fairyland in an evident state of rapture. He wrote lyrically of what he saw.

"I am unwilling to dwell too long on the beauties of the grand canal and yet it is necessary to say something of all this crowd of islands in the midst of which are planted so many pagodas, differing from each other, both in date and in the style of their architecture, some simple and square, with three or four storeys not unlike some of our village steeples, only each of the storeys is marked by a little blue projection turned up at the extremity; others are hexagonal, octagonal, with four, six, seven storeys. They are all beautifully situated, appearing as it were to start from the water, amidst fine masses of trees, either alone or close by the house of some mandarin. Not must I forget these veils of bamboos, of such brilliant colours, which cover the water in every direction, and bend to every breath of air."

Borget's vessel passed "on the left an island with a little battlemented fort, in the middle of which is a pagoda" and then "we at last caught site of the mountains behind Canton, and arrived at the entrance to the district of Honan.

"We were immediately surrounded by boats rowed by Europeans, who have only this means of taking a little exercise. We entered the right arm of the river, on which Canton is situated, and I very soon perceived, through a forest of masts, European flags, and afterwards the factories themselves."

On September 20, Borget wrote of the landing in Canton and his first sight "of the little spot which the sublimity of the Emperor has conceded to the barbarians"—the European quarter.

He tells us that "the space allotted to the factories consists merely of a strip of land gained from the river, measuring not more than seven or eight hundred feet in length by about three or four hundred feet wide. In front of each factory, at the top of a high mast, is displayed the national flag—English, French, American, Dutch etc.

"This is the only part of the city where a European is permitted to walk; and as it is at all times crowded by Chinese of every rank, the foreigner gains little by this tolerance. They therefore generally content themselves with taking the air on the roofs of their houses when they cannot sail along the canals, which are, it appears, considered neutral ground.

"The European habitations front the south, and are bounded on the east by a ditch or inlet from the river, over which there is a bridge leading into the street which passes behind the factories. All the hongs have communications with the river by means of stairs from which the merchandise is shipped. On the west are Chinese houses bounded by a canal without outlet, but which is always crowded with boats. The hongs are divided into three separate groups by two thoroughfares; one called China Street, the other Hog Lane. In the western group, on which New Street opens, and which encloses four factories, is the French hong, which does not front the place; it is situated between the Spanish hong and that of a Chinese merchant trading with Europeans. The middle division contains the Danish, American, English and Austrian hongs, with heavy graceless fronts."

Borget wrote that it was "the hong of the East India Company which far outshines all the others, with its projecting terrace supported by columns. It is indeed the finest and the most pretending of all the foreign buildings in Canton. It has a little garden enclosed by a wall on each side, and a palisade on the river."

He also mentions another building belonging to a "merchant to whom the Chinese have given the nickname of the old iron-toothed rat." This was presumably a reference to the Scottish trader, William Jardine, who began life as a surgeon, graduated to trading, made his way to India and later Canton where he met a certain James Matheson, whence the famous partnership resulted. Borget's rendition of the Chinese nickname, however, was not quite accurate. The contempt with which the Chinese viewed his firm's involvement in the opium trade would seem to have been partly offset by their admiration for the way he unflinchingly withstood a heavy blow on the head while presenting a petition at the city gate in Canton. Thus he became known as the "iron-headed old rat".

Ever curious, Borget left the security of the foreign residences to walk through the streets. He wrote in one of his books: "The artist who, sick of the sight of small hawkers and artisans who come to ply their trade in front of the factories, wishes to leave the confines of the prison assigned to the Europeans, to which they have repeatedly to return, can only venture with extreme caution into the fabulous maze of streets in the environs of Canton.

"They are so narrow, so lively, so noisy; the passers-by are so numerous, so busy, and the hawkers so indifferent about bumping into you with their loads, that it is hard to find an empty corner where one can sit with an album."

He reports on the passing scene: "To whichever side of the city one turns one's steps, in whichever street one walks or in whichever place one stops, there are certain trades and certain individuals one never misses seeing."

He then described the itinerant barber with all his paraphernalia—including wash basin, wooden stool with drawers containing combs, razors, tweezers, ear-cleaners and eye-lustre. He tells of seeing the barber plaiting the long black hair of women. Nearby was a locksmith; further on there were mobile food stalls with large umbrellas, and a fortune teller.

"Around him a crowd gathers while credulous customers follow one another without pausing. Alas, they are trying to shut their eyes to the present in the hope of a better future," he wrote.

However, it was the temples which attracted him, and as with Macau's temple of Ma Tso Kok Borget found Canton's counterpart equally intriguing. He visited it several times and discovered to his surprise that far from it being crowded there was complete solitude.

"The noise without was so great and the silence of the temple so solemn that I believed myself transported to another world. The impression was such that for a moment I fancied that the wicket, once shut, would not open again and that I was separated for ever from the rest of the world."

In this almost other-worldly atmosphere Borget sat down to sketch.

In one of his tours he came across a house whose walls enclosed a great tree. He wrote "When they began to build they found it growing in the line of their wall; anywhere else it would have been cut down at once, but here they know that a tree does not spring up in a day, and they therefore sacrifice it only to a pressing necessity; they therefore included it in the building, and thus saved a good many bricks to the proprietor, who has besides the enjoyment of a magnificent shade, a thing by no means to be despised in so hot a climate.

"I began to sketch this place, but the immense crowd which pressed round me obliged me to suspend my work for a time, till, thanks to a mandarin who passed near me in his black carriage, and whose cortege of tom-toms, flags, and all the other insignia of his dignity, diverted the general attention."

76

On other days during his brief stay, he trudged over rice paddies, studied trees, inspected temples, admired pagodas and repeatedly took to the river to make a closer inspection of a fort, or an island or a junk.

He was shown the Dutch Folly—an island fortress which Borget said was built about a mile from the foreign factories. "It is an oval enclosure, with embattled walls, above which are seen the dragons and dolphins which surmount the roofs of houses standing under some fine trees.

"No one is allowed to enter in the enclosure, which owes its name to an attempt which the Dutch made to establish themselves on the Chinese territory—an attempt which failed, to their great mortification. At one period, when they carried on a most extensive commerce with China, they requested and obtained possession of this little island, but after landing a great number of boxes, the suspicions of the Chinese were aroused. They made them open one, and inside was found a quantity of warlike stores.

"The Chinese government immediately retracted the permission, and the Dutchmen were obliged to abandon the island, chagrined and ashamed at having been discovered.

"Since that time, the name of the Dutch Folly is given to this fort which they intended to arm and doubtless to defend against the Chinese—as if a foreign nation could, at five thousand leagues distance from their native home, establish itself by force among a people so homogeneous.

"As to the other little fort, which is two miles lower down the river, I never could learn why it was called the French Folly, for it was not built by a Frenchman. It is like the other, oval and embattled with some buildings, and a square tower in the middle. It is so picturesque, from whichever point it is seen, that the first time that I visited the spot, I brought away three different sketches."

One of Borget's many regrets was that he could not learn to read the Chinese characters which everywhere taunted him. "My ignorance of the Chinese language has been to me a cause of much regret, for nothing would have interested me more than to be able to read this mark of the character of the inhabitants."

Finally, towards the end of his stay in Canton he took a river trip of almost 15 miles through the delta country "and while my companions talked and smoked I sketched without relaxation, for there is constantly some new feature in the landscape which I have not seen elsewhere."

His tour took him along the canal of Honan and he tells of reaching a bridge "which was soon crowded with gazers, and nothing could be more laughable, I assure you, than the multitudes of heads rising gradually above each other on the steps of the bridge—for here all the bridges are made like stairs—some covered with hats of every form, and others sheltered by parasols, every face bearing an expressive desire to see the *fanqui*.

"A little to the right, we saw an elegant building, painted in the brightest colours, the balconies of which were so slender, so light—the little columns so weak—that it seemed as if a breath could have upset it; nevertheless, in spite of those appearances, every thing is solid. This bamboo must be a marvellous kind of wood; we have nothing like it in Europe: here it is used for every purpose.

"The curtains of the lower rooms being open we had an opportunity of forming an idea of the extraordinary luxury which reigns inside of this house. It was fitted up with a profusion of lustres, lamps, and revolving lanterns, very much ornamented. The windows were supplied with silken blinds, and the little awnings which shaded the balconies were placed by every storey all round the house.

"Here the young fashionables were strutting about, some smoking long pipes, the others fanning themselves in the most grotesque and amusing attitudes. The house is a celebrated resort, where the gourmands of the city come in search of pleasure, and taste all the dainties of the country, seated, as with us, at little isolated tables."

But Borget was obviously not impressed with the fare. "I admit," he writes, "that the smells which reached us did not make us envy their enjoyment, for the strong odour of fat and of oil of burnt resin, which constantly streamed out of the kitchens, would effectually keep at a distance any European who might be tempted to go thither in search of the delicacies of the table."

If the restaurant did not excite Borget and his friends, the scenery outside beckoned them on. As they continued their journey by boat the canal narrowed and led them "under the arches of a very high bridge, about four feet wide. It afterwards again widens, and on its banks we saw a charming pavilion, surrounded by gardens, enclosed by a balustrade, covered with vases of flowers. A stairway leads to the door of this house, which is said to belong to one of the salt merchants, who are reckoned amongst the richest traders of China."

They then passed house boats and Borget tells of seeing "one of these magnificent boats in which the Chinese have accumulated all the comforts of life. It was of immense size, and although we only saw it cursorily, we could nevertheless judge of the richness of its decorations and furnishings. The owners, who were in the cabin, were richly dressed, and a crowd of servants encumbered the deck. The boat was moved forward by pushing it with a long bamboo, applied to the shoulder, and touching the bottom of the canal.

"After a sail of three hours, we landed near a temple for they are everywhere to be seen and we ascended a large and magnificent plateau. The view from this spot was very pleasing. We were behind Canton and could see its pagodas through the trees and sometimes overtopping them . . .

"To this place ought the artists of Canton to come to gather inspiration for nothing can equal the beauty of the landscape."

The serenity with which Borget wrote of this seemingly idyllic period in Canton contrasted strangely with the ferment that was building up and of which he was well aware.

As a Frenchman he could perhaps well afford to take a detached view of a problem that was largely of the British merchants' making but the opium trade, during the closing months of 1838, was assuming increasingly serious proportions.

Under the zealous campaign of the specially appointed Chinese Commissioner, Lin Tse-hsu, the Kwangtung Governor, Teng Ting-chen and a highly feared judge, Wang Ching-lien, the Chinese authorities were making a desperate bid to stamp out opium-smoking and its importation by foreign merchants, principally (thought not entirely) British.

We are not certain of the date Borget actually left Canton. A surviving sketch is dated 1839 and the earliest published letter bearing a Macau dateline is January of that year. He could therefore have remained in Canton until just after the new year.

A drawing from Borget's Canton period exhibited at the 1849 Salon in France, was entitled "A disgraced Mandarin begging for mercy under the walls of his old residence." There is regrettably no indication of the mandarin's identity. But during the month of December two major incidents occurred in Canton which Borget must have heard about since one involved a riot in which a number of foreigners took part.

The other incident concerned James Innes, a British merchant who was smuggling opium into Canton. A Chinese official on December 3, 1838 caught labourers unloading the contraband opium into Innes' factory. They were arrested, almost certainly tortured and they named Innes as the owner though the opium had been transported in an American ship.

Innes and the captain of the vessel *Thomas Perkins* were ordered to leave within three days (later amended to 10). The Chinese Hong merchant who stood security for the ship was put into the stocks with a heavy wooden collar (or *cangue*) around his neck.

The other Hong merchants rallied to his defence and threatened Innes that they would pull his factory down on top of him if he did not obey the order to leave. The threat was not carried out, however, and tension subsided until the December 12 incident, which was far more serious.

Then, the authorities decided to pursue their intimidation of the foreigners by bringing a criminal condemned to death for selling opium, into a public square under the windows of the foreign factories.

They drove a wooden execution cross into the ground directly under the American flag. At that point, 70 or 80 foreigners gathered to stop the execution. When they moved in and smashed the cross and tore down an official tent, a riot developed. It was only stopped when two Americans, Gideon Nye and William Hunter, slipped out of the American factory via the roof, crossed to an adjoining building, and managed to reach the residence of the chief Hong merchant, Howqua, who in turn called on the authorities to restore order—a request to which they responded immediately.

Borget's picture could well have been of the first incident (or an imaginary drawing based on the two incidents.) Hong merchants were in many cases known to have been awarded minor positions in the mandarinate in return for the financial support they gave the Government. This entitled them to wear their buttoned hat, the colour of the button denoting the rank.

The Borget picture shows a splendid mansion in the background and the disgraced official with the torture clamps still on his fingers.

It appears from the picture that he is about to be tied to a post. In the foreground, two women are kneeling. A mandarin, wearing his hat and ceremonial jacket, presides over the proceedings.

Borget did not include this picture in his 1842 album of sketches of China. Perhaps he felt his readers would have little or no interest in what many French people regarded as a minor Anglo-Chinese squabble.

That they would themselves be drawn into the Chinese wars some 20 years later was not then apparent.

SKETCHES OF CHINA AND THE CHINESE

PARIS
Publié par GOUPIL et VIBERT, Éditeurs,
Boulevard Montmartre, 15 et rue de Lancry, 7.
1842.

Frontispiece of Borget's book *Sketches of China and the Chinese*

◄ A trading junk lying in the
river off Canton

▼ Dragon boats near French Folly
Island on the river between
Macau and Canton

Chinese camp on the outskirts of Macau

Hong Shang

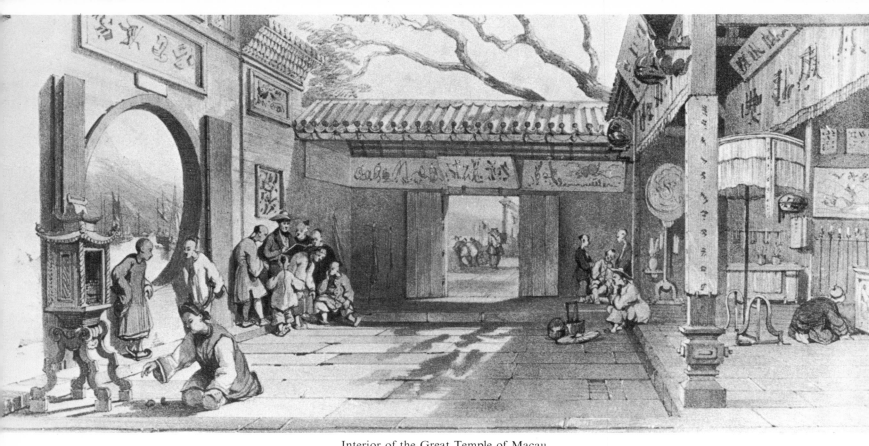

Interior of the Great Temple of Macau

Chapel of the Great Temple of Macau

Grave and village, with Hongkong harbour in the background

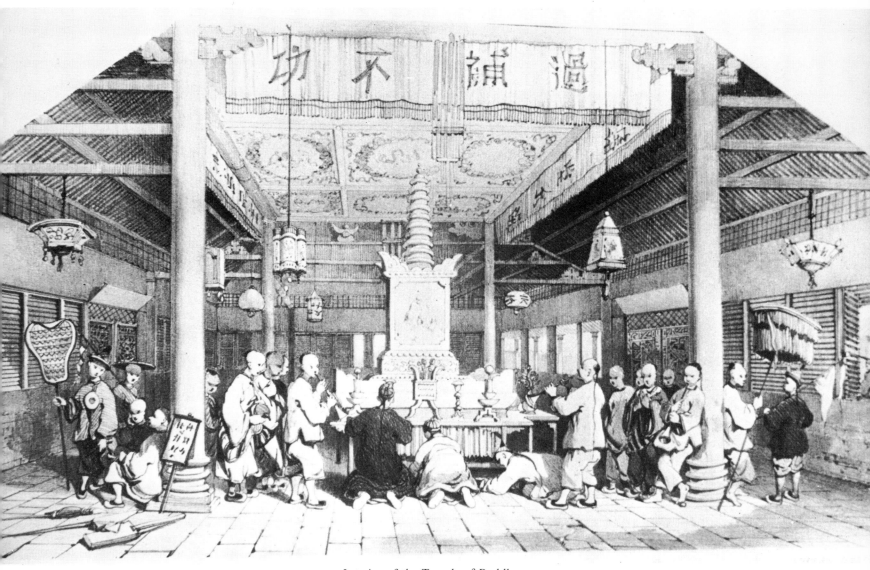

Interior of the Temple of Buddha

◄ Old temple near the Macau border

▼ Temple, pagoda and village on the banks of a canal near Canton

A junk travelling along a canal near Canton

Homes of the poor, Macau

Temple and canal at Honan

Home of a wealthy salt merchant on a canal at Canton

Village near Canton ►

Sampan dwellings. Bay of Kowloon ▼

Interior of a fort, island of Nam O

Temple of Buddha, district of Honan, Canton

Portuguese church and Chinese street at Macau

MACAU, MANILA, INDIA

AUGUSTE BORGET'S stay in China lasted more than 10 months, four of which he spent visiting parts of the Kwangtung and Fukien coast and the Pearl River delta, including Canton, and in the remaining six months he settled happily in Macau.

It is clear from surviving letters that he enjoyed life there, for in a letter he wrote to Honoré de Balzac on his return to France he referred to a business transaction which almost brought him a fortune.

"Do you know, my dear friend, that I saw financial success very nearly within my grasp? Had it not been for the contraband trade in opium there would have been no war: had there been no war, I would have left Macau with 40 or 50,000 francs . . . "

The nature of his business is not revealed. Certainly he is unlikely to have made such a sum from painting or sketching, and we are left to guess how one so inexperienced in the complexities of the China trade could have amassed such an amount.

In a book published in Paris after his return he reveals he had made friends with an unnamed "wealthy British merchant". This merchant "whose kindly welcome I shall never forget, offered to take me along to Marseilles where he had rented a house in which a room was ready for me."

It is possible that his connection with this merchant had led to business discussions but there is nothing to suggest that Borget embarked on his world trip to make a fortune. He was apparently comfortably provided for in Paris, undertook a business deal to help him on his way from Le Havre to the United States, worked briefly in New York but spent the rest of his time sightseeing and sketching.

He found Macau so pleasant that he hoped at one stage to "stay for a much longer period". He gave up his nomadic existence and settled down, took lodgings in an apartment or house with a terrace, and engaged a servant. Had hostilities not intervened it is possible that George Chinnery, the British artist who had been living in Macau since his self-exile from India in 1825, might have found his reputation as a scenic painter seriously challenged.

It is tempting to speculate on the relationship between the two artists. We know that while in Macau they exchanged pictures. This evidence came to light in America when a picture formerly owned by Mr Gideon Nye, an American resident of Macau and Canton whom we met briefly in the previous chapter, was found to have a label declaring it to be a "scene near Macao: by M. Borget—as an interchanged gift to Mr Chinnery."

More recently, shorthand references to Borget have been found in Chinnery's drawings and one refers to a "design of Mr Borget". A picture of a young man dated 1839, carries the shorthand inscription "Mr Borget" (see page 123).

From our knowledge of how warmly Borget responded to the presence of Rugendas, the Bavarian artist in Chile, and how anxious he was to profit from this association by improving his techniques, it would seem likely that Borget and Chinnery met frequently. We know that in Macau and India, Borget sketched scenes almost identical to those by Chinnery suggesting that he saw many drawings by the British artist, or watched him at work.

At the age of 30, Borget realised he still had a lot to learn—with little if anything accomplished in the way of portraiture—while Chinnery, then a mature 64 and with a wealth of experience and a diversity of talent in every medium of painting, water colouring and sketching, would have much to offer in advice and help. Chinnery had, after all, helped a number of pupils in both India and Macau, among them Mrs Maria Browne in Calcutta, Sir Charles D'Oyly in Dacca and Calcutta, and Dr T. Boswell Watson and Marciano Baptista in Macau.

There is one other clue to contacts between the two artists. Borget's biographer, David James, refers to a series of "rapid little sketches of every-day life which are typical of the artist's stay in China." This could have been a habit he picked up in Macau and it was also a very notable feature of Chinnery's own work-style, thousands of which survive to this day.

The link is admittedly tenuous but there are so many similarities in the sketching styles of the two artists that it is difficult to accept these were a coincidence. There is, furthermore, a remarkable liveliness in Borget's China sketches, a wealth of detail and a considerable improvement in his drawing of human figures, lending additional weight to the belief that he benefited from frequent meetings with Chinnery.

Borget met at least one other painter in China, a Chinese artist who undertook commissions for portraits and landscapes from foreign businessmen, seamen and tourists, and who proved at one time a serious competitor to George Chinnery. His name was Kwan Kiu-chin or, as he was known to most of his customers, Lamqua. He established his studio in Canton and Borget has left us a picture of this three-storey Chinese-style tenement, with its signboard "Lamqua, handsome face painter" above the main entrance.

Although a highly regarded painter himself, Lamqua employed about 20 workmen and produced most of his pictures on a production-line basis, each worker contributing according to his own specialisation— one painting faces, another clothes, another background, another special effects. It is likely, however, that Borget regarded Lamqua with no more than amused curiosity; certainly he would have learnt little more than how to turn "art" into a successful retail business.

For Lamqua sold his pictures at about one-fifth the price of Chinnery's and as a consequence built up a large clientele.

Like Chinnery, Borget was endlessly fascinated by all he saw in Macau, including the winding cobble-stone streets of the Portuguese section, the "inextricable labyrinth of the part inhabited by the Chinese", the profusion of domestic animals and the miserable destitution of what Borget called the "aquatic streets".

Ever curious Borget was quick to explore the city. He found in some parts that "the houses move about as well as the inhabitants. There, where perhaps last night I found no opening, a street now stretches itself out; and the street by which I formerly passed is now altogether closed. How many sketches have I lost from putting off their completion till the morrow."

Equally amazing to Borget was the way pigs wallowed in pools of water which covered parts of the Chinese quarter— "the size to which these animals increase is almost fabulous; and their numbers, which are nearly incredible, sufficiently testify the preference the Chinese give to their flesh over every other.

"The rich indeed prefer that of cats and dogs, and sometimes even rats, but everyone has his taste."

The aquatic streets which Borget referred to were villages of old junks and sampans, hauled ashore.

"It was impossible," he wrote, "for a European, even when he sees it, to imagine how so many people can exist in such a narrow space."

He then described how they came to exist. "The first comers take possession of the ground, and there they place their worn-out boat, which can no longer float on the water. Those who come next place around the boat stakes of wood, thus forming a sort of stage over the heads of their predecessors, either by hoisting up their boat, or when they do not happen to be so rich, by forming a flooring, which they surround with mats, and cover in by a roof of the same materials.

"Still poorer individuals follow, who, having neither boat nor materials to form a flooring, nestle them-selves in the intervals between the older habitations, and there suspend their hammocks; and uncertain as the tenure of this locality is, it yet serves for the accommodation of a whole family. Often a single ladder is sufficient for five or six such habitations, and yet there is neither any right acquired by one, nor dependence felt by another. Each habitation has its little balcony, from which are displayed mats or rags of every description."

Not satisfied with a distant view of these settlements, he wrote to his friends in Paris that he visited a number, climbed up the rickety ladders to their balconies "and notwithstanding the smallness of the space, there were flowers everywhere; it afforded me great pleasure to find some poetry among so many privations.

"They are so crowded together that they can scarcely find in such pigsties room enough to erect the domestic altar, which is nevertheless not wanting in any of them . . . . Every morning and night they offer tea to the divinity and light the little red wax lights."

He was cheered to find that despite the miserable state of these nooks of five feet square, as he called them, every face he encountered "beamed with joy" and "whenever they have a moment to spare, they amuse themselves by playing with dice.

"At the least cry, from every dwelling, which before seemed deserted, are pushed out innumerable heads and one cannot help wondering where they all came from, and how so many people can possibly hide themselves in such a space."

Borget's drawings and lithographs of sights like these are among his finest.

And in the town of Bourges in France there is an oil painting of majestic proportions in which Borget showed his true skill as an artist. It was this painting that was bought by King Louis-Philippe at an exhibition in Paris in 1841.

This is the scene outside the Great Temple of Macau—the temple of Ma Tso Kok on the south-eastern tip of the peninsula. He described this as "the greatest marvel I have yet seen . . . almost daily I visit this temple either in the morning when all is shadow or in the evening when every stone and tree and roof reflects the sun, or at mid-day when the extreme heat obliges me to seek its grateful shade.

"Viewed as an object of Chinese art, everything in the disposition of the edifice is admirable; its arrangement, its picturesque situation amidst rocks and trees, as well as the numerous ornaments by which it is enriched . . . I am assured that nowhere else in China is there to be seen a more remarkable edifice, and I believe it, so superior is it to anything I have elsewhere seen."

His other sketches of Macau include a somewhat unusual view of the city from a promontory on the south-east tip looking north to Penha hill, and views of churches.

Two others call for comment. One was a burial scene which was one of the most picturesque published in his book *Sketches of China and the Chinese*. He recalls that he was alone in his study in May, 1839, and "felicitated myself on the unusual tranquility which reigned in the exterior roads. I was no longer deafened by the incessant noise of the gongs and the guns of war junks, which watch the city on that side. Everything seemed asleep."

However, he heard the noise of tom-toms. He rang for his servant to ask the cause—"being told that a very rich personage who had died some days before was about to be buried, and that the cortege would very soon begin to move, I hastily dressed myself and proceeded to the place, very curious to witness the ceremony."

He wrote in some detail and with great perception of the funeral procession. He described their clothing as "being coarser in proportion to the nearness of their relationship.

"The women, who uttered piercing cries and unable when unsupported to stand steady on their little feet, kept close together to keep themselves from falling.

"When the procession began to move, each of the ladies was lifted by a female servant who, not without much fatigue and several stoppages by the way, carried them on their backs to the place of burial.

"The bearers of the lanterns and the flags led the way, followed by a multitude of musicians playing on a kind of sharp-toned clarinet. Behind them came the coffin, preceded by a long banner of red silk, on which were inscribed in gold letters the titles and quality of the defunct, and with the end of which the eldest son of the deceased covered his face as they proceeded.

"Then followed the women, borne as I have already described. In the rear were carried three tables covered with fruit, dishes of meat and a large roasted pig."

At the burial place "the coffin was placed on trestles, and all the relatives kneeled round it, striking their forehead and responding to the verses chanted by the bonze, the wailers all the time uttering the most doleful cries.

"During this ceremony which lasted a couple of hours, the servants remained behind and laid aside their indifference only when the procession preparing to resume its march homeward they had once more to take up their loads.

"The tables were brought away untouched, nothing being left near the grave but a few crumbs, some wax lights and joss-sticks.

"Although very much inconvenienced by the sun which was very hot, I did not leave the position I had selected till my sketch was finished. The situation was magnificent: on my left lay the Fort of Guya; on my right the Monte, and in front the town which the sea laves on both sides; while beyond stretched out Lapa and the other islands until they disappeared in the distance."

Borget's home was, from his description, on the eastern side of the harbour. As the weeks passed relations between the Chinese authorities and the British traders steadily worsened. The firing of guns from Chinese war junks, which Borget referred to earlier, was part of the psychological pressure that Commissioner Lin Tse-hsu's forces were applying to the small community of foreigners in Macau.

In Canton, the British merchants had been forced to surrender more than 20,000 chests of opium to the Chinese authorities and on May 24, three days after Borget had sketched the funeral scene—all British subjects left the factories in Canton for Macau for the last time.

War was only a matter of weeks away and life was becoming increasingly difficult for British residents even in Macau as, under the prompting of Commissioner Lin, servants began to leave and shop-keepers became rude and unco-operative.

But Borget was not yet ready to quit. In mid-June he heard that Commissioner Lin's Tartar troops had set up camp on the other side of the Barrier Gate which served as the border between Macau and China.

Showing considerable courage he decided to visit the camp. He wrote in a letter to France "you may well imagine that I was unwilling to lose the opportunity—the only one it might be that I shall ever have—of inspecting a Chinese encampment, even although I was told that they had maltreated some foreigners who had gone near them.

"Their tents, which exactly resemble ours, were ranged in a single line, with the exception of that of the chief. In the only two which were open I saw stands of arms ornamented with shields, on which were painted the head of a tiger.

"The soldiers exercised themselves in shooting at a target with bows and arrows, and they really showed much skill.

"In one corner a sentinel kept watch over a poor fellow who was in a *cangue*; close by sat a chief tranquilly smoking his pipe.

"The only similarity between a Chinese encampment and a European one is that both have clean and well-made tents. What a difference is there between our active soldiers, always in motion, with their well-fitting uniform and martial air, and those pacific men embarrassed by their unwieldy garments, armed with lances, pikes and matchlocks.

"What would become of that empire, if it should engage in a conflict with a European power? Besides when one sees these soldiers cooking their rice and eating it, one can easily understand that in this employment they follow the tendency of their organisation more closely than in occupying themselves with soldiership."

The letter was dated June 20 and Borget left soon after to avoid the inevitable conflict. The British residents followed two months later and spent most of the rest of the year living on board merchant ships anchored in Hongkong harbour.

The troops that Borget saw in the camp then held a massive victory parade through the streets of Macau, escorted by a contingent of Portuguese soldiers.

Borget took passage on board a ship which sailed for Manila, arriving there on July 28, just seven days after Commissioner Lin had ordered the Chinese sub-prefect of Macau to withdraw all Chinese servants from British residents.

He remained in Manila sketching scenes of the Pasig River (which runs through the old quarter of the city), churches and native dwellings, as well as the surrounding countryside in Luzon, until August 5. From there his ship sailed for India, via Singapore and the Straits of Malacca, arriving in Calcutta where he disembarked. Although he does not mention this part of his tour in his album, he did exhibit a painting of a Burmese temple in France in 1846.

During his stay in India, Borget settled briefly in Calcutta where he produced a number of outstanding sketches and once again they show a strong Chinnery influence, possibly the result of seeing drawings made by the British artist during his stay in that city 15–20 years earlier. Borget's biographer, David James, believes these "splendid drawings, the finest of his stay in the Far East, show his delight amid the landscapes and architecture of India.

"We no longer find the rapid little sketches of everyday life which are typical of the artist's stay in China, but instead a number of large, detailed and serene drawings of mosques and minarets, of river banks shaded by palms, banyan trees and bamboo, graceful compositions of Hindu temples, intertwining vines and sacred cows contemplating the infinite."

Borget was no admirer of the English way of life in that city. He scorned the "magnificent areas in Calcutta where the English have established their splendid homes" and wrote in his book describing his world tour, that "I am not going to fill the pages of my album sketching the facades of their palaces."

He continued: "Rather than their pseudo-Greek architecture I prefer the narrow, winding streets of the old city. The rags of the impoverished people living under the sway of a company of merchants seemed to me more picturesque than the astounding luxury of their conquerors, and their customs more interesting than those of the English who are invariably the same in all parts of the world where they are established.

"I often go at sunset to the banks of the river, bristling as it is with masts, and at the time of day when they bathe, establish myself on my carriage, while one of my bearers holds a large sunshade over my head; there I sketch the most obscure corners of this populous area and I never fail to discover some picturesque ruins.

"I return by Clive Street, parallel to the river and one of the major arteries of the city, which takes me right opposite my residence. On occasions I sketched the old bazaar, the interior of which would keep an artist busy for more than 15 days. How many miserable souls are buried in this old palace which perhaps soon will cease to exist . . .

"Opposite the colonnades on which hang these rags, and under the terraces of a house which one reaches by climbing a steep staircase, an old fakir has walled himself in. However, we were allowed to make use of a small opening by which devotees and women who come to pray, can pass him the food that he needs.

"This one, at least, did not inspire any disgust or horror such as his fellow creatures, fanatic by profession and who take pleasure in living in filth and imposing on themselves by pride, laziness or foolishness, the most horrible torture; vile race, idiotic to the point of making your stomach turn—which fortunately one finds only in India."

After Calcutta, Borget travelled widely in India and if the locations given on his pictures which he subsequently exhibited in France are to be believed he crossed from Assam in the East to the Hooghly River with stops at cities such as Patna, Benares, Mirzapoor and Allahabad at the confluence of the Jumna and Ganges Rivers. These are all dated 1840.

This part of his visit, however, has not been described in his album. He was taken ill in India and he decided to return direct to France. Again there is no mention of the homeward journey and he reappeared in Paris in the summer of that year.

Thus ended a memorable, exciting and highly productive voyage. His artistic vision had certainly widened and his technique had benefited greatly as much from the variety of scenery he had sketched and painted, as from the influence of artists like Rugendas in Peru and Chinnery in Macau.

In 1840 he was 32. Borget had developed considerably in these years away from Balzac and Zulma Carraud, his close friends in Paris. He had learned to stand on his own, had had time to reflect on life, and his inherent goodness and kindness, which Balzac had often noted, was seeking new forms of expression.

MUSÉE DE LA ROCHE ISSOUDUN

A selection of Borget's sketches

Gate of a temple at Macau

A scene of Bengal

A sketch of a valley near Honolulu

Banana palms and bamboos

HOME-COMING

IT IS uncertain whether it was his illness in India or a homesickness for France that prompted Borget to end his world tour in 1840. Perhaps it was a combination of the two. He had been away for more than three and a half years, part of the time in the company of his French friend, Guillon, but for the last two years on his own.

A sociable and likeable person such as Borget, however, had no difficulty in making new friends along the way and often on his travels he moved about with others, except when he was on his sketching expeditions when he naturally preferred to take his own time and be on his own.

But his long absence from France had no doubt stirred a wish to see his family and return to his circle of friends in Paris. He was also curious to see how Balzac, already well-known and highly respected before Borget left, had progressed in his career as a writer.

Still in his early 30s, Borget was keen to discover whether his world tour had advanced his stature as an artist and to test the market for his landscapes of remote and exotic countries far from the shores of France.

Borget wrote to Balzac announcing his return in August 1840, telling him he had "innumerable drawings made in all parts of the world."

Zulma Carraud had told Borget that it had become very difficult to see Balzac, so he wrote saying: "How will I be received by you? If you are living in complete solitude, if you refuse to be visited, how will you know that it is I who knocks on your door, I, your old friend, I, the confidant of many of your sorrows? Goodbye, expect to find me as far as you are concerned the same as the day I left."

Balzac replied by the next post: "My good, old and reliable friend, at all hours, at any moment, you will find the door open and a room yours. I have thought a lot about you; Mme Carraud will confirm this. As far as my condition is concerned everything is worse. Friendship, yourself, debts, work, everything has grown . . . I cannot write at great length about this to you dear Borget. Come my dear and you will be received like the day before you left . . . Goodbye my dear, my very dear . . . "

Balzac in that year was as usual preoccupied with his own affairs. Still interested in publishing despite the debt of 45,000 Francs he had incurred in taking a major interest in the *Chronique de Paris* he attempted in 1840 to launch a periodical called *Revue Parisienne*. It ran to three issues, mainly written by himself. He returned to another hectic period of writing which lasted until 1843 and then his pace began to slacken as personal worries crowded his life—ill-health, financial problems and Madame Hanska's continued postponement of their marriage.

Borget was busy with re-establishing himself, completing paintings and arranging drawings to be exhibited in salons and he had his own plans to publish books based on his letters and sketches sent to France during his world tour.

Having exhibited a picture of the Italian countryside in the Salon of 1836, Borget regularly entered pictures from his world tour from 1841 to 1850 and succeeded in attracting the interest of both the public and the connoisseur as an oriental artist.

In addition to Paris he exhibited in provincial cities and towns such as Boulogne, Nantes, Montpellier, Toulouse and Limoges.

Perhaps his greatest triumph was in selling one of his masterpieces to King Louis-Philippe in 1841 for 1,200 francs (just 200 francs less than the Impressionist painter, Camille Pissarro, earned for one of his masterpieces 50 years later). And according to contemporary accounts, the King may well have bought others.

At the 1843 Salon, Borget won a gold medal for his picture entitled "A Calcutta Street" and at this stage his sketches and paintings were widely discussed—and criticised. He was at the height of his fame.

Borget decided that the time was right to publish some of his pictures he had made during his voyage, and he entrusted the lithography to Eugene Ciceri of Paris and the publishers of his first book, *La Chine et Les Chinois,* were Goupil et Vibert of Paris.

Recalling the interest shown by English friends in Macau, he also decided to have his letters translated and the book published in the same year by Tilt and Bogue of Fleet Street, London, in association with Ackermann and Co of the Strand and Henry G. Bohn of Covent Garden (32 plates, lithographed in two tones, 28 pages of text). He dedicated it to his royal patron King Louis-Philippe.

The book should have enjoyed a brisk sale. Not only were the pictures some of the best he had done but the quality of the lithography was outstanding. Moreover, his friend Balzac reviewed the book in the journal, *La Legislature,* in October of that year.

Nor did he confine it to a single article but wrote four long instalments with extensive extracts from the book, and of course gave his own rambling discourse on the Chinese and China, discussing their religion, poetry and way of life.

If there was far more of Balzac than Borget in the review that was inevitable. Borget had noticed his extreme egoism even before he began his world tour; fame and success in the meantime had aggravated the condition.

Balzac began his article thus: "A Frenchman in China. An artist! An observer! Who is he? Well, he is a native son of one of the most stagnant and least progressive parts of France, a painter of landscapes born at Issoudun in the plain of Berry. Sometimes chance takes the appearance of the impossible; that is its fatuity."

If his words sounded somewhat mocking and patronising they at least concealed Balzac's deeper feelings about Borget's talents. At the beginning of their friendship Balzac sensed in him the makings of a great artist and said of him in his early 20s "he will be great all of a sudden." But this view changed after he returned: "I fear he is no genius and we have so much talent that another one will not be noticed." Moreover he once spoke of his friend's "detestable Chinese paintings which Louis-Philippe buys."

If the remark is considered a trifle caustic, it was a view shared by others. The critic, Charles Beaudelaire wrote that "Borget is not a great artist. But his talent is very respectable. As one says in his part of the country: he is a very capable artist."

It was perhaps Borget's over-concentration on oriental life that caused the critics to tire of him. Beaudelaire in reviewing his work in the 1845 Salon commented: "Always views of India and China. No doubt they are very well done but they are regrettably too precisely souvenirs of a journey or accounts of customs. The paintings of Mr Borget make us regret the China where the wind itself, as Mr Heine says, has a comic quality about it as it blows on the bell-flowers and where nature and man cannot look at each other without laughing."

A year later the tone was different. "Mr Borget has crossed the borders of China and has shown us Mexican, Peruvian and Indian landscapes. Without being an artist of the foremost category he has a brilliant and easy colour. The tones are fresh and pure; with less art and in thinking of himself less as a landscape artist and painting more simply as a traveller, Mr Borget would obtain perhaps some more interesting results."

Undeterred by these criticisms, however, Borget followed up the publication of his China drawings with another book in 1845 entitled *Fragments d'un voyage autour du monde* this time with only 12 lithographs and 12 pages of text published by Desrosiers.

In the same year Borget provided 215 illustrations for a book entitled *La Chine Ouverte* by 'Old Nick', a pseudonym for Emile Forgues (published by H. Fournier, Paris). These wood engravings do not compare in quality with those published in his own books. They have a somewhat whimsical quality but show how thoroughly Borget had studied life in China.

Most are signed "AB" and while the majority were drawn from nature (or a good memory) he has included a number of regions of China which he did not visit, such as Nanking and the Great Wall. Borget in these instances based his drawings on sketches by other artists.

On the whole they provide an illuminating insight into life in China at the time and he was certainly the most qualified artist in France to carry out this assignment.

So highly were his pictures regarded that when an English clergyman, the Rev G.N. Wright, put together a book in 1843, on "the scenery, architecture and social habits of that ancient empire, China", he commissioned Thomas Allom to provide the drawings, at least seven of which were direct cribs of Borget pictures without any acknowledgement.

Borget also drew an imaginary sketch of the arrival in Macau of the French Ambassador, M. Théodose de Lagrenée, in 1844, for the signing of France's first commercial treaty with China, which was published in the *Journal d'un voyage en Chine* by Jules Itier in 1848. Clearly his first-hand knowledge of China, if not his reputation as an artist, was greatly respected in his own country as well as in Britain.

In 1841, the journal, *L'Artiste*, had reported: "It is possible to take a very pleasant trip to China by visiting (Borget's) studio. This young artist has already shown his gifts as a faithful draughtsman and colourful author by revealing the customs, arts and monuments of the Chinese people. But it is especially in Mr Borget's studio that one can gain an intimate view of this peculiar corner of the world."

In between his publishing and his exhibitions, Borget continued to visit and correspond with his friends, Balzac in Paris and Zulma Carraud who had by now moved to Frapesle. And there is no doubt that whatever Balzac felt about his talent as an artist, he was still the same, loyal and dedicated friend, "Le Bon Borget."

In 1836, when Borget was preparing for his world tour, Balzac had written *The Atheist's Mass*, a book he dedicated to him. It was in this book that Balzac had created the character "the good Bourgeat", a poor water carrier from Auvergne, whose labours, savings and affection were devoted to the medical studies of a young man named Desplein who later became the most illustrious surgeon in the country.

There is no reason to believe that Balzac's appreciation of all Borget did for him ever waned. Indeed there were many times in the years between 1840 and Balzac's death in 1850 that he regretted seeing less and less of his old friends. His last letter from the Ukraine to Zulma Carraud in March, 1850, in which he announced his marriage, ended by asking her to send his kind remembrances to "good Borget".

It is possible to understand this tenderness Balzac felt for his younger friend for they shared a link not only in the appreciation of art but in lyrical expression. Borget had published in 1850 several articles about his world tour in the journal *L'Art en Provence* in which he showed himself to be an able writer with an attractive style.

In these articles, Borget mentions his ordeal in a China Sea typhoon, his distress at the plight of the South American Indians and the Polynesians who were being persecuted by supposedly civilised colonists, and he was particularly severe on the attitude of certain American missionaries in the Sandwich Islands (later Hawaii).

He wrote of the great dignity of the Indian and Malayan labourers who loaded and unloaded cargo from ships at his ports of call in contrast with the cursing, swearing members of the crew who supervised their work.

"Some of these men are so marvelously handsome that one could believe them to be the remainder of a vanished race. My artistic imagination took pleasure in dressing them in silk, in throwing rich cashmere shawls over their shoulders or winding turbans around their heads, and then transporting them to palaces which I built for them in the midst of the lush vegetation of Bengal. Sometimes I could not help comparing them, naked as they were, to the small number of European sailors who were giving them orders and cruel blows.

"The advantage was not in favour of the latter whose wine-reddened faces, stupid expressions, raucous voices and coarse gestures formed a painful contrast with even the least resigned and least interesting face to be found among their victims."

As one writer, Romain Guignard, says: "Throughout these articles and in his correspondence with his friends, we familiarise ourselves with the winning character of this artist who was independent, original, with an extreme tenderness of feeling, faithful and frank in friendship, always ready to help and render service, thoughtful and tender, loving music, with a passion for flowers and all in all justifying the high praise in the simple epithet 'Le Bon Borget.'"

The year 1850 was a climactic period for Borget. Balzac's death was a severe blow to their close friendship and at the same time the Carraud family left for Nohant en Gracy, about 20 miles from Issoudun.

Borget moved to Bourges, the capital of his native province of Berry, a city he knew well from his school days. Zulma Carraud kept up a correspondence with her friend but Borget was undergoing a profound change in his outlook to life and although he continued to sketch and give lessons he took less interest in art and stopped exhibiting at major salons.

Mme Carraud wrote to a friend in 1855 that Borget was still in Bourges but his love of flowers was taking all his time and money. He was short of cash and "he wants to sell his green-house in order to remove this hourly temptation."

Not yet 50, Borget seems to have begun a semi-retirement and a retreat into his inner-self. There is no clear indication of Borget's attitude to religion in his earlier life.

Various authorities suggest that in his early manhood he came to profess atheism; the title of the book Balzac wrote for, and dedicated to him, *The Atheist's Mass* is significant in this respect. Yet Balzac was a most perceptive observer of human nature and his frequent references to "the good Borget" indicate that he saw a deep faith and devotion below this superficial atheism.

Like many Christians who renounce the church but embrace its deeper teachings Borget as a young man wore his atheism like a fashionable habit. And as his life progressed he was to exchange this for one of piety and humility.

111

We can see in his letters from South America and China that he was above all a humanist with a strong social conscience, who experienced great distress at scenes of suffering, cruelty and hardship. And in his later years he underwent a period of mental and moral torment, a rejection perhaps of his early, carefree and somewhat uninhibited life style. He rebelled against acquisition of material things, his home, his many souvenirs of his world tour. He denounced Balzac's affectionate epithet "Le bon Borget"—"why call me good? No one is good, unless it is God himself."

He plunged into a new vocation of devotion and charity to the poor. Having given up his house, he moved into the wing of a large home belonging to the des Meloizes family and there spent the rest of his life.

As one friend noted "one did not know what to admire more—the vivacity of his faith or the heroism of his charity or his spirit of self-denial and mortification."

In 1856, he joined the Society of St Vincent de Paul. Romain Guignard, writing on Borget at this time, tells us that "he lived only to give service to the unfortunate, going as far as to distribute as alms the last crumbs of his possessions."

He went about Bourges in a long cape with a hood—not a religious vestment but a shepherd's habit from Issoudun—visiting the sick and dying.

Was it a true conversion, or a deep and intensely disturbed reaction to his former way of life? There seems no reason to doubt that Borget, of whom Balzac had once predicted "all of a sudden he will become great" had found that greatness comes not from superficial fame as the world knows it but from the discovery of the relation between man and his creator, and the demand this in turn imposes.

As Borget had freely and happily given his life to art, travel, friends and his own comfort, he now gave it to his God. He joined the lay Society of St Francis Xavier where he served first as Vice-President and later President until his 60th year. Where before he had revelled in the writings of his friend Balzac and other contemporary novelists, now he devoted himself to religious books and the Bible.

He wrote about this new existence in a notebook which survives him: "One must love poverty as well as the poor. If the outcry of a sick body in agony moves you to compassion, how much more so should the sighing of a soul?"

Though he continued with his art in his attic studio giving lessons to talented children, Borget destroyed the last relic of his old life when he burnt his correspondence with Balzac and Mme Carraud.

The secret of this deep and intimate relationship he thus took with him to the grave. Borget died in the town of Chateauroux only a few miles from his birthplace, after a long illness on October 25, 1877. His death certificate describes him as a man of independent means, and was signed by his brother, Pierre, and his nephew, Alfred. His funeral, as befitting one who had in his last years given so much to the church, was held in the massive and majestic cathedral at Bourges.

At some period in his life, Borget's teacher, Gudin dedicated a painting to him thus: "To my pupil in painting, and my master in charity".

For at the last Borget had found his true vocation.

Borget, from a photograph taken late in life.

THE ALLOM COPIES

In 1843, the publishing house of Fisher, Son & Co, Newgate Street, London, published a four volume edition of *China, in a series of views, displaying the scenery, architecture and social habits of that ancient empire,* written by a clergyman, the Rev. G.N. Wright and illustrated by Thomas Allom, an architect.

It would appear that neither Wright nor Allom had visited China though Allom had illustrated a similar book on the Turkish empire.

Allom's drawings were not entirely imaginary, however. He based them on "original and authentic sketches" by artists who had visited China, among them William Alexander, Lieutenant White of the Royal Marines, and other artists whose drawings were brought back to England by Sir George Staunton, following official visits to China.

One of the artists whose works Thomas Allom copied but did not acknowledge, was Auguste Borget.

On the following pages, the Borget originals and the Allom copies are reproduced.

Allom possibly saw the Borget pictures in his English edition of *Sketches of China and the Chinese* published a year prior to Wright's four volume account.

The result is that Allom's charming though fanciful pictures are today more widely known (and more frequently republished) than Borget's.

Borget's sketch of the Great Temple of Macau

Allom's sketch of the same scene

Borget's sketch of the interior of a temple

Allom's sketch of the same scene

Borget's sketch of the courtyard of a temple in Macau

Allom's sketch of the same scene

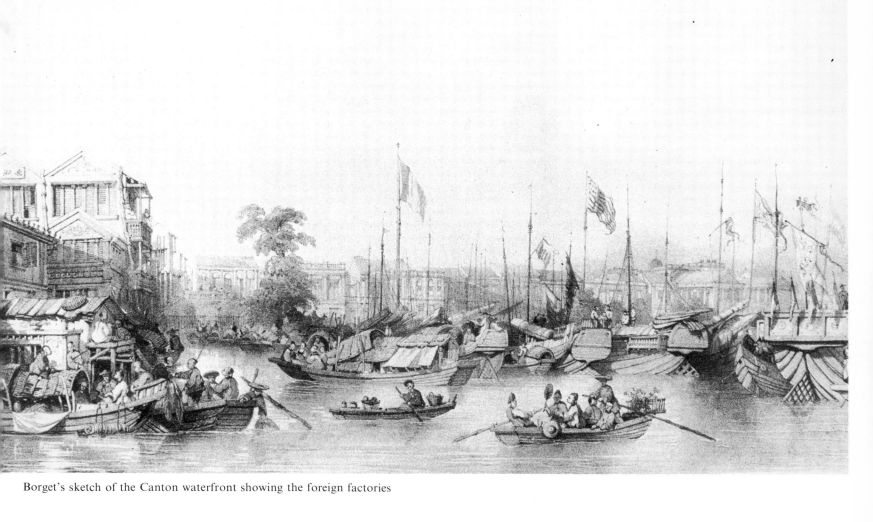

Borget's sketch of the Canton waterfront showing the foreign factories

Allom's sketch of the same scene

Borget's sketch of the aqueduct, Hongkong

Allom's sketch of the same scene

Borget's sketch of the harbour and Hongkong island

Allom's sketch of the same scene

Shortly before this book went to press, a collector of prints and drawings living in Kowloon, Mrs M. Austin, received from a dealer in England a photograph of a drawing by the British artist, George Chinnery, showing a young man leafing through a book. Chinnery lived in Macau from 1825 until his death in 1852. The picture was dated 1839, the year Auguste Borget left Macau on his return to France. There is a shorthand note under the date which says "Mr Borget". This sketch can be compared with the Rugendas sketch of Borget on the title page.

BIBLIOGRAPHY

Beeching, Jack: *The Chinese Opium Wars,* Hutchinson, 1975.

Borget, Auguste: *Fragments d'un voyage autour du monde,* Desrosiers, Moulins, 1845.

Borget, Auguste: *Sketches of China and the Chinese,* Tilt & Bogue, London, 1842.

Coates, Austin: *Prelude to Hongkong,* Routledge & Kegan, Paul, London, 1966.

Chang Hsin-Pao: *Commissioner Lin and the Opium War,* Harvard University, 1964.

Eitel, E.J.: *Europe in China,* Kelly & Walsh, Hongkong, 1895.

Forgues, P.E.: *La Chine Ouverte,* H. Fournier, Paris, 1845.

Gould, S.C.: *Balzac,* Encyclopaedia Britannica, 1973.

Guignard, Romain: *Personnages et monuments d'Issoudun,* H. Geignault et fils, Paris, 1949.

Guignard, Romain: *Balzac et Issoudun,* H. Geignault et fils, Paris, 1946.

Hibbert, Christopher: *The Dragon Wakes,* Longman, London, 1970.

James, David: *The Artist Traveller,* Gazette des Beaux Arts, Vol 46, 1955.

Moorhead, Alan: *Darwin and the Beagle,* Penguin, London, 1971.

Wright, Rev. G.N.: *China, in a series of views, displaying the scenery, architecture and social habits of that ancient empire,* Fisher, Son & Co, London, 1843.